عصـــــر الأثـــــر الخافـــــت

THE SILENT AGE OF SINGULARITY

THE SILENT AGE OF SINGULARITY

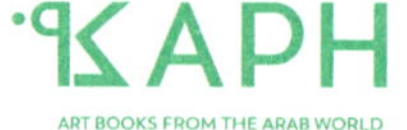
KAPH
ART BOOKS FROM THE ARAB WORLD

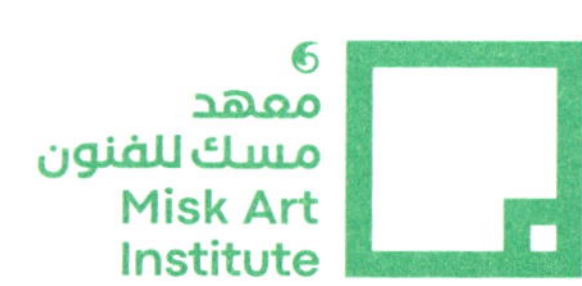
معهد
مسك للفنون
Misk Art
Institute

عصر الآلة الخافت

THE SILENT AGE
OF SINGULARITY

كتيـــــب المـــعرض

EXHIBITION CATALOG

نص التقييــم الفنــي CURATORIAL TEXT

عصــــــر الأثـــر الخافــــت
THE SILENT AGE OF SINGULARITY

بســمة الشـــثري وآرام العجاجـي
Basma Alshathry and Aram Alajaji

ص. p. 7

مقــال ARTICLE

ثقافــــــة الإنترنــــت
ALTERNATIVE CULTURES

أ . د عبدالله الغذامـــــ
Prof. Abdullah Alghathami

ص. p. 13

مقابلــــــة INTERVIEW

الفنانــــة د. إيمــــان الجبريــــن
THE ARTIST DR EIMAN ELGIBREEN

آرام العجاجـي
Aram Alajaji

ص. p. 19

الفنانــــون وأعمالهـــــم
ARTISTS & ARTWORKS

ص. p. 27

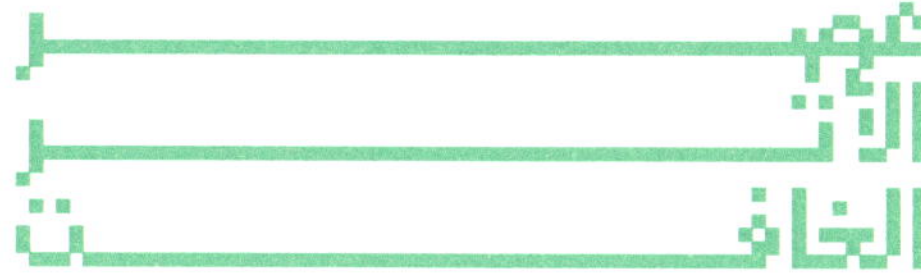

THE SILENT AGE OF SINGULARITY

بــسمة الشـثري وآرام العجاجـي
Basma Alshathry and Aram Alajaji

In an era where technological progress unfolds at an unprecedented pace, the ripple effects of these advancements resonate across societies worldwide. Satellites, television, and the Internet have emerged as transformative forces, ushering in an age of information dissemination, cultural exchange, interaction, and global interconnectedness. The 1960s stand out as a pivotal decade in the evolution of digital technologies, laying the foundation for the technological landscape we navigate today. Initially conceived to interconnect computers, the inception of the Internet in the United States during this time marked a paradigm shift. Tim Berners-Lee's groundbreaking invention of the World Wide Web in 1989, publicly unveiled in 1991, allowed a multitude of users to traverse a virtual realm within a few years. The Internet swiftly embedded itself into the fabric of daily life, marking its emergence as a turning point in the twentieth century. Evolving beyond a mere tool for communication, the Internet has since become an indispensable facet of modern existence. From passive observers on desktop computers, individuals have metamorphosed into users engaging with the digital realm around the clock via personal devices.

شكّل عقد الستينيات من القرن الماضي فترةً محورية في تطـور التقنيـات الرقمية التي أسسـت للمشـهد التكنولوجي الذي نعيش فيه اليـوم، فالإنترنت صُمّم في البداية لربط أجهزة الكمبيوتـر، إلّا أنه أحدث منذ نشأته في الولايات المتحدة نقلةً نوعية هائلة، حيث أن الاختراع الثوري لشـبكة الويب العالمية على يد تيم بيرنرز-لـي فـي عـام 1989، وإتاحته للعامّـة في عام 1991، مكّـن ملايين المسـتخدمين مـن الدخول إلى العالم الافتراضي في غضون بضعة أعوام، وسـرعان ما تغلغلت شبكة الإنترنت في جميع تفاصيل الحياة اليوميـة، الأمر الذي مثّل انعطافاً جوهريّاً عند نهاية القرن العشرين. ومنذ ذلك الحين، تطور الإنترنت إلى أبعد من مجـرد أداةٍ للتواصـل، وصار عنصراً أساسـيّاً لا غنى عنـه في الحيـاة الحديثة، وتحـوّل الناس من مراقبيـن سـلبيين لأجهـزة الكمبيوتـر المكتبيـة إلـى مستخدمين نشطين يتفاعلون مع العالم الرقمي على مدار الساعة عبر الأجهزة الشخصية، وفي ظل تسارع وتيرةِ التقدم التكنولوجي على نحو لم يسبق له مثيل، وترّدد أصداء التطـورات التكنولوجيـة المتلاحقة عبر المجتمعات فـي جميع أنحاء العالـم، وتمتع الأقمار الصناعية والتلفزيون والإنترنت بقوة تحويلية افتتحت عصر انتشـار المعلومات وتوسّـع المبـادلات الثقافية وارتفاع مسـتويات التفاعل وتعزيز الترابط العالمي.

the presentation grapples with several key themes, including connectivity and interconnectedness, perception and identity, creative expression, the concerns of technology, and the overload of information.

In the digital age, connectivity and interconnectedness have become central to our lives. With the rise of the Internet, artists have harnessed new avenues of communication, circulated information, reached global audiences, and transcended geographical boundaries, thus challenging traditional notions of knowledge circulation. Nam June Paik saw television as both muse and canvas, envisioning the related satellites as windows to explore the world from our homes. Similarly, Ahmed Mater reflects on how these satellites opened doors to new cultures, diverse ways of thinking, and broader exposure, leading to a transformation in his creative process. Mahdi Aljeraibi associates connectivity with nostalgia, using abandoned school desks to highlight the evolution of communication and the connections of a bygone era. Even though connectivity is heavily relied upon, it is not universally available—Ibrahim Abumsmar explores this through his commentary on losing digital connectivity.

After increased exposure, technology has reshaped how we see the world, both literally and figuratively, raising questions about perception and identity. Faisal Samra and Omar Alzahrani explore the tension between identity and reality by inviting viewers to confront the disconnect between their true selves and the facades they present to the world. Eiman Elgibreen addresses themes of globalization and identity, as she looks at the digital manipulation of perception and the authenticity of online identities. Bennett Miller poses questions about the enigmatic nature of perception, reality, and truth through the use of artificial intelligence. Khaled Makhshoush

وعنـد التأمـل فـي الترابـط بيـن تاريـخ البشـرية والابتـكارات التقنيـة، يظهـر نمـطّ واضـح يتمثل فـي تسـارع الاختراعـات، بدءاً من البوصلة إلى المحركات البخاريـة والطائـرات وصـولاً إلـى الإنترنـت، ونظـراً لمـا يشـهده عالمنا اليـوم مـن تغييـرات لا تُضاهى وتقـدّم منقطع النظير، فلا شـك أن إيقاع التطورات المسـتقبلية سـيزداد تسـارعاً؛ كان عالـم الفيزيـاء والحوسـبة جـون فـون نيومان قـد طرح فـي عام 1958 مفهـوم «التحـوّل الجـذري»– وهـو فرضيـة تتكهّـن بمستقبلٍ يـؤدي فيـه تطور المعلومـات وتكنولوجيـا النانـو والبيولوجيـا، إلـى ظهـور ذكاء عـام اصطناعـي يدفـع البشـرية نحو «تحـوّل تقني جـذري». بهـذا المعنـى، يشـير عنـوان معـرض «عصر الأثر الخافت»، إلـى فتـرةٍ مـن التحولات العميقـة التـي تحـدث بـكل هـدوء تحـت سـطح الحيـاة اليوميـة، حيث يتوجّه العالـم نحو الاندماج الشـامل بيـن الأفـكار والثقافـات والخبـرات، ونعني بالأثـر الخافت، تلـك التأثيـرات الخفيّـة والقوية في آن واحـد، والمتمثلة فـي كيفية تواصلنا مـع العالم وإبداعـه وفهمه، والمؤديـة بالضرورة إلـى تغييرات هادئـة، ولكنها هائلة على صعيد التجربة الإنسانية، ومـع بـزوغ عصر الإنترنت وتلاشـي الحـدود بيـن الخصوصيـة الفردية والاسـتهلاك العـام، ظهـرت مسـاحات واسـعة ومواتية لتنامي الإبداعات وتزايد المتغيـرات، الأمر الـذي أدى إلى ظهور مـا يُمكن أن نسـميه فن مـا بعـد الإنترنت.

إن (فـن ما بعد الإنترنت) يُجسد حركةً يلعب فيهـا الإنترنـت دوراً جوهريّاً في تشكيل التفاعلات الاجتماعية والمعاييـر الثقافيـة والتعبير الفني، فمن خلال مجموعة من الأعمال التي اسـتجابت للتحول الثقافـي الـذي أحدثـه الإنترنت. يحتضن معـرض «عصر الأثر الخافت» عشـرين عمـلاً لفنانيـن عملوا علـى استكشـاف مشـهد مـا بعـد ظهـور الإنترنت، ويقـدّم رؤى مختلفة حـول دور التكنولوجيـا فـي تشـكيل المجتمـع وتأثيرهـا علـى التعبيـر الإبداعـي فـي العصـر الرقمـي، وتأتـي هـذه الأعمـال ضمـن مجموعـة متنوعة من الوسـائط، كالرسم والأعمال

As we reflect upon human history interwoven with technological innovation, a pattern emerges: the acceleration of invention, from the compass to steam engines, airplanes, and the Internet. The present day stands unparalleled in the magnitude of change and progress it witnesses, hinting at an accelerated trajectory for future advancements. John von Neumann, a physicist and computer scientist, introduced the concept of "singularity" in 1958—a hypothesis envisioning a future where advancements in informatics, nanotechnology, and biology culminate in the emergence of artificial general intelligence (AGI), propelling humanity toward a "technological singularity." The title of the exhibition, *The Silent Age of Singularity*, suggests a period of profound transformation occurring quietly, beneath the surface of daily life, as the world moves toward a merging of ideas, cultures, and experiences. This "silent" phase evokes the subtle yet powerful shifts in how we connect, create, and comprehend the world, leading to a delicate but monumental change in human experience. With the dawn of the Internet Age, the boundaries between individual privacy and public consumption have blurred, creating a space filled with the potential for innovation and change to grow.

Art post-Internet encapsulates a movement where the introduction of the Internet to daily life plays a central role in shaping social interactions, cultural norms, and artistic expression, and it encompasses works that respond to the cultural shift brought about by the Internet. Exhibiting the works of twenty artists, *The Silent Age of Singularity* explores the intricacies of the post-Internet landscape, presenting a diverse range of perspectives on how technology shapes society and influences creative expression in the digital era. Featuring an array of mediums, including painting, sculpture, video, photography, and installation,

التركيبيــة والفيديو والتصويــر الفوتوغرافي، ويتناول المعرض من خلالها عدداً مــن المحاور الرئيسية: الاتصال والترابط، الإدراك والهوية، التعبير الإبداعي، التحديـات التــي تثيرهـا التكنولوجيـا، والكـمّ الهائل مـن المعلومات.

وقــد أصبـح الاتصـال والترابـط فـي العصـر الرقمـي مــن العناصـر الأساسـية فـي حياتنـا، ومع ظهـور الإنترنت، أبـدع الفنانون في تسـخير السـبل الجديـدة للتواصـل وتـداول المعلومـات والوصول إلـى الجماهيـر العالميـة بشـكل يتجـاوز الحـدود الجغرافية، الأمـر الذي مكّنهم من تجاوز المفاهيم التقليديـة لتناقل المعارف. فقـد رأى نام جون بايك في التلفزيـون مصدرَ إلهام ولوحـةً فنيـة، وتصوّر الأقمـار الصناعيـة كنوافـذ لاستكشاف العالم مـن منازلنا، وعلى نفس المنـوال، يتأمل أحمد ماطر في الأقمـار الصناعيـة التـي فتحت الأبواب على الثقافات الجديـدة وطـرق التفكيـر المتنوعـة، موسـعةً آفاق المعرفة، مـا أحدث تحـولاً فـي عمليتـه الإبداعية، وعلـى صعيـد آخر يربـط مهـدي الجريبـي الاتصال بالحنيــن إلى الماضي، مسـتخدماً طـاولات التلاميذ المُستغنى عنها لتسـليط الضوء على تطور الاتصال والترابط، ويستكشـف إبراهيم أبو مسمار من جهته، ظاهـرة الاعتمـاد المتزايـد علـى الاتصـال رغم عدم توفّـره بعـد للجميـع، متخيّـلاً حـدوث توقـف في الاتصـال الرقمـي.

لقد وسّعت التكنولوجيـا مـن آفـاق الاطلاع وأعادت تشكيل رؤيتنـا للعالـم، حرفيّـاً ومجازيّاً، ما يطرح إشكاليات الإدراك والهوية، وفي هذا المعرض يستكشـف فيصل سـمرة وعمر الزهراني التناظر بين الهويـة والواقع من خلال دعوة المشاهدين للنظر في الانفصال بين ذواتهم الحقيقية والواجهات التي يقدمونها للعالم، وتتناول إيمان الجبرين موضوعات العولمـة والهويـة، ملقيةً الضـوء علـى التلاعـب الرقمـي بـالإدراك وموثوقية الهويات عبر الإنترنت، ويطـرح بينيـت ميلـر التسـاؤلات بشـأن الطبيعـة الغامضـة لـلإدراك والواقـع والحقيقـة باسـتخدام الـذكاء الاصطناعـي؛ بينمـا يعيـد خالـد مخشـوش

expanding the visual language of abstract art. DAVID HOCKNEY has created works on the iPhone and iPad, marking a pivotal phase in his exploration of how technology intertwines with artistic expression. SOUFIANE IDRISSI and MOHAMMED CHROURO integrate artificial intelligence to transform colors, forging new paths in contemporary painting. SAEED GAMHAWI traces the progression of human innovation from primitive carvings to artificial intelligence, illustrating how technological advancements have evolved.

These rapid advancements lead us to consider the evolving role of artists in a landscape submerged in technological progression. In navigating this terrain, artists are not only adapting to technological changes, but also redefining digital innovation in art. This speculative horizon prompts contemplation on the prospect of Creative Singularity—a realm where digital technology unlocks new forms and approaches for artistic creation. Thus, the question may not be whether artists will compete with machines, but how they will influence and transform technology to further enrich creative expression in this digital age.

تصور المناظر الحضرية المحلية متأثّراً بألعاب الفيديو، ليشكّل العناصر المألوفة ولكن من منظور غير مألوف، متطرّقاً بذلك إلى كيفية تحويل العوالم الرقمية لإدراكنا للواقع.

ومع انتشار الشاشات في كل مكان، وامتدادها في كل حدب وصوب، يُعاد تعريف علاقتنا في استهلاك الفن، إذ توضع جميع المعارف العالمية في متناول اليد، ولكن لكل ذلك ثمنًا يتمثل في الكمّ الهائل من المعلومات والصور التي يتعامل معها الفنانون، وفي الفيض العارم من المرئيات والبيانات المتاحة في المشهد الرقمي الراهن تنظر آنيا سليمان وأيمن يسري ديدبان في آثار هذا الكمّ الهائل، ويستكشفان موضوعات القلق والهوية والذاكرة في سياق الترابط العالمي الفائق، ويتأمل تركي القحطاني ذلك السيف ذا الحدين المتمثل في الاتصال الرقمي الذي يعزز التواصل من جهة، ولكنه يقصفنا من جهة أخرى بوابل لا هوادة فيه من المعلومات البصرية التي تتجاوز حدود الإفراط والإسراف في كثير من الأحيان.

وتمتد المخاوف التي تثيرها التكنولوجيا إلى ما هو أبعد من فوائدها المباشرة، لتشمل قضايا الهدر التكنولوجي وتآكل الأشكال التقليدية لحفظ الذاكرة، حيث نجد في المعرض جون سالفيست متأملاً في مستقبل حفظ الذاكرة في ظل التحول الرقمي المتسارع، وبجانبه يستعرض زياد كعكي أدوات المراقبة الحديثة وتعدّيها على الخصوصية؛ بينما ينتقد منير فاطمي الهدر التكنولوجي واستبدال تناقل المعارف المادي الملموس بالتناقل الرقمي، متأمّلاً في التقادم التكنولوجي وحفظ الذاكرة، وفي المخاوف الأوسع تجاه دور التكنولوجيا في إعادة تشكيل التجارب والعواطف الإنسانية.

ويأتي اتساع آفاق التعبير الإبداعي نتيجة للتطور التكنولوجي، الأمر الذي سمح للفنانين بالإقدام على مغامرات جديدة، فنجد سامية حلبي وقد قامت بتعليم نفسها البرمجة وطورت لغةً تصويرية استخدمتها لتحريك الأشكال والألوان والأصوات،

reimagines local landscapes influenced by video games; these terrains offer a nuanced perspective on familiar elements while reflecting on how digital realms transform our perception of reality.

The ubiquity of screens and the accessibility they provide redefine our relationship with art consumption, making universal knowledge accessible at our fingertips. Yet, this comes with a price: an overload of information and imagery that artists tackle, which addresses the overwhelming abundance of visuals and data in today's digital landscape. Ania Soliman and Ayman Yossri Daydban examine the effects of this overload, exploring themes of anxiety, identity, and memory within the context of a hyperconnected world. Turki Alqahtani reflects on the double-edged sword of digital connectivity: it enhances communication, but it also bombards us with relentless, often excessive visual information.

Concerns surrounding technology extend beyond its immediate benefits, encompassing issues such as technological waste and the erosion of traditional forms of memory preservation. John Salvest contemplates the future of memory preservation in an increasingly digital world. Ziad Kaki paints the capability of modern surveillance and its erosion of privacy. Mounir Fatmi critiques technological waste and the shift from tangible to digital knowledge transmission, while also engaging with technological obsolescence and the preservation of memory, reflecting broader concerns about how technology reshapes human experiences and emotions.

Advancements in technology have expanded the horizons of creative expression, allowing artists to explore new ventures. Samia Halaby taught herself to code, developing a pictorial language that she has used to animate shapes, colors, and sounds,

موسّعةً بذلك اللغـة البصريـة للفن التجريـدي، أما ديفيـد هوكنـي فقـد ابتكـر أعمـالاً علـى أجهـزة الـ iPhone وiPad في ما شـكّل منعطفاً حاسـماً في استكشافه للتشـابك بين التكنولوجيا والتعبير الفني، وفـي حيـن يتبنّى سـفيان إدريسـي ومحمد شـرورو الذكاء الاصطناعي لتحويل الألوان والتمهيد لمسارات جديدة في الرسم المعاصر، ويتتبع سعيد قمحاوي تطور الإبداع البشـري من المنحوتات البدائية وصولاً إلـى الـذكاء الاصطناعـي، مسـلطاً الضـوء على مدى تقدم التطورات التكنولوجية.

وكل هذه التطورات السريعة تدفعنا إلى التفكير فـي تغيّـر دور الفنانين فـي العالم المغمـور بالتقدم التكنولوجي، فالفنانون لا يكتفون بالتكيّف مع التغيرات التكنولوجية فحسب، بل يعيدون أيضاً تشكيل ملامح الابتـكار الرقمـي فـي الفـن، ويقودنا التأمـل في هذه الآفاق إلـى النظر في إمكانية حـدوث «تحوّل إبداعي جذري» حيث تفتـح التكنولوجيا الرقمية الأبواب على مصاريعها أمام مختلف الأشكال والأساليب الجديدة في الإبداع الفني، وبهذا قد لا يكون السؤال ما إذا كان الفنانون سيتنافسـون مع الآلات، بل كيف سـيؤثرون على التكنولوجيـا ويوجّهونها لإثـراء التعبير الإبداعي في هـذا العصر الرقمي.

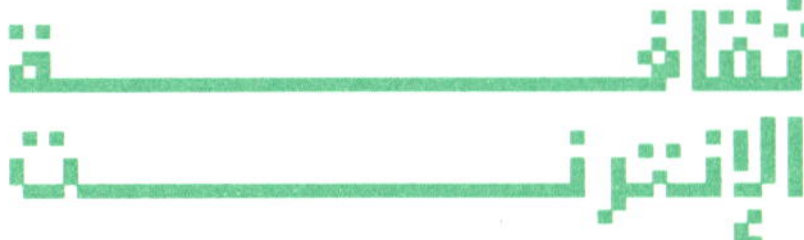

ALTERNATIVE CULTURES

أ. د عبدالله الغذامـــي

Prof. Abdullah Alghathami

Since the dawn of humanity, people have dreamed of a means that could ferry them across space and time, immortalizing their thoughts and memories. Egyptian poet Ahmed Shawqi (1868–1932) referred to this concept as "a second life":

One's heartbeat says to them,
Life is minutes and seconds
So upraise its remembrance beyond your death
For remembrance of a human is their second life

This second life may extend farther than a mere "other life." Indeed, human beings have always aspired to have lifespans that could stretch so far as to be recognized across time and space—beyond the reaches of the human voice. They even go beyond the amplifiers, perched daises, and those first methods for expanding the scope of communication to relay voices past the sensory domain.

The human brain is a network, and it has been one since the very beginning. Cultural remains bear the only traces from which we may glean the pathways of the brain and its relationship to the invention of things that serve our practical lives. These objects have enabled us to conceive of the

منـذ مطلع زمـن الثقافة البشـرية والإنسـان يحلم بثقافـة تعبر بـه المكان والزمان وتخلّـد فكره وذكره وهو ما سـمّاه أحمد شـوقي بالعمر الثانـي بقوله:

دَقّاتُ قَلبِ المَرءِ قائِلَةٌ لَهُ
إنَّ الحَياةَ دَقائِقٌ وَثَواني
فَارفع لِنَفسِكَ بَعدَ مَوتِكَ ذِكرَها
فَالذِكرُ لِلإنسانِ عُمرٌ ثاني

ولعـل هـذا العمـر الثانـي هو عمـر ممتـد أكثر من كونـه مجرد عمـرٍ ثانٍ، فالإنسـان بأعمـار متمددة يتسـع لها فضاء الاستقبال الزماني والمكاني باتساع يتجـاوز ما يبلغه صوته المحـدود أو حتـى المكبر الصوتي أو المنبـر المرتفع فـوق الـكلّ، وهمـا قد كانا أولى وسـائل الإنسان لتوسـيع دائرة التواصل فتحمـل الصوت إلـى أبعد مـن مجاله الحسـي.

والعقـل البشـري هو عقل شـبكي مـذ مطالع شـواهده، والشـواهد الثقافية وحدها هـي العلامة التـي نسـتطيع عبرها التعـرف على مسـارات العقل البشـري وعلاقتـه مـع فكـرة (الاختـراع)، أي اختراع أمـور تخدم حياتـه الواقعيـة وتمكّنه مـن تصور ما ليس فيه، مثل فكرة الطيـران، حيث الإنسـان كائن أرضي ولا يسـتطيع جسـمه الطيران، ولكنـه يظل يتصور نفسـه يطير في منامه وينتقـل بين الأمكنة، إمـا تشـوّقاً لشـيء أوهربـاً من آخر. وظلـت الفكرة

In this regard, it must be noted that the invention of writing is what enabled human beings to reach across time and space in the first place. Shawqi notes that "remembrance of a human is their second life" because text outlives its author. It is a material of lasting memory, a place where ideas are kept alive so long as there are people to read them. Lifespans thus range between human life expectancy and further durations, the latter of which are gained via means that immortalize people's links to their contemporaries and their successors. This keeps them among us, as though they are alive whenever a text bearing their name is read.

The arrival of the Internet intensified, facilitated, and accelerated communication. This massive invention marked a momentous cultural and scientific milestone. It has also become a pivotal component of the economy, one that has changed the rules and regimes of thought and planning. With this change to our systems of intellect and expression, the Web has, moreover, impacted politics and security—and political discourse itself has become a virtual one, formulated to correspond to countless modes of reception. Political messaging, for example, is no longer aimed at one class of people, but rather, it is open to all who can receive the messages. This has affected our means of articulation, given our awareness that anything we say could have global reach and permanence as a historical record of image, sound, and body language, elements complementing the written text, which itself would be spoken and viewed. This interplay of formats has led to the creation of an alternative language with its own sophistication and fundamentally distinct devices.

With this immense spread of information has come one of the most dangerous challenges that humanity faces: hacking. The idea of warfare has transformed from one in which destructive weaponry

تلاحقه لتصبح أمنيةٌ. وكانت محاولة عباس بن فرناس أبرز مثالٍ على محاولة الطيران، وتمثل لها صيغةٌ تشبه صيغة الطائر، ولكن محاولته فشلت بموته، وإن كانت قد أشعلت الرغبة في طيران الجسد. وقبل ابن فرناس كانت فكرة الطيران خيالاً أدبياً كما في بساط الريح. وهذا التخيّل عن وسيلة طائرة يمتطيها الإنسان فتطير به، هي التي تحققت بعد قرون مع الأخوين رايت، حيث تمكنا من تحويل بساط الريح إلى صناعة حديدية طائرة. ومن هنا طار الإنسان عبر وسائل صناعية تحمله حيث يشاء وبلغ حدود الفضاء وما زال يحلم بالمزيد.

وهنا وصل الإنسان إلى تحقيق واحدة من أهم خيالاته، ولكنه ظل يتشوق إلى تمديد أنظمة اتصالاته مع البقاء في مكانه، فحلُم بأن يمتد مادياً إلى أبعد من مكانه، فاستخدم الحمام الزاجل كي يبعث بمشاعره وغير مشاعره إلى جهات بعيدة، ثم وصل إلى جهاز البرقية التي ألغت الحمام الزاجل، فأوصلت الرسائل بطاقةٍ أدقَّ وأضمن. وتتابعت ابتكارات الإنسان عبر الراديو ثم التلفاز ثم الفاكس ثم أن وصل إلى الإنترنت، وكلها وسائل تواصل تربط الإنسان مع غيره، وتحقق له مبتغياته في الاتصال. وجاء ما يسمى بالواقع الافتراضي، وهو امتداد للواقع الحسي. وجاءت معه مواقع التواصل الاجتماعي التي خلقت بيئةً اجتماعية تضاف إلى البيئة الواقعية، فتعددت حيوات الإنسان وتعدد وجوده بصيغ متشابكة قد تختلط علينا أحياناً بين واقع نلمسه وواقع ذهني نستقبله ونتعامل معه.

وفي هذا الصدد لابد من الإشارة إلى اختراع الكتابة، لأن الكتابة حققت للإنسان التمدد عبر الزمان والمكان معاً. فالمكتوب يعيش بعد موت صاحبه، ولذا قال شوقي (فالذكرُ للإنسانِ عمرٌ ثاني)، لأن الكتاب هو مادة دوام الذكر، ومن ثم يبقى الفكر حياً ما وُجد له قارئ يقرؤه. ومن هنا تتعدد أنواع العمر بين العمر المتوقع للكائن البشري والأعمار التي يكسبها عبر وسائل تخلّد

yet-inexistent, things such as the idea of human flight. Despite our terrestrial nature and corporeal incapacity for flight, people kept dreaming of it—of traveling from place to place in yearning or escape. The incessant thought of it became a coveted wish, epitomized in the ninth century by Andalusi inventor Abbas ibn Firnas (809/10–887), whose avian-inspired attempt ended in failure and death. However, it also further kindled our longing for flight. Prior to ibn Firnas, the idea of human flight was the subject of literary fantasy, as we can see in tales featuring the magic carpet. This fantasy about a means of flying to transport humans would be fulfilled in the early twentieth century by the American Wright brothers, who managed to transform the notion of the magic carpet into an actual flying machine. Since then, people have flown to their destinations of choice via mechanized craft, eventually crossing the boundaries of outer space and still dreaming of more.

Humans thus achieved one of their most remarkable dreams, but they remained eager to extend the reach of their systems of communication beyond the immediate reach of the individual. Homing pigeons, for instance, were used to relay both sentimental and non-sentimental messages to distant locales. Then came the telegram, which did away with birds by delivering communications using a more reliable and precise source of energy. Human innovation continued, ushering in the radio, television, fax, and, ultimately, the Internet—all means of interconnection and communication in service of human objectives. Then came a so-called "virtual reality," an extension of sensory reality, and with it, social media, which created a social ecosystem alongside the real world. The lives of humans have thus multiplied, as has their presence across interwoven formats in a mixture of a tangible reality and a mental one with which we perceive and interact.

له علاقتـه مـع المعاصريـن والآتـين مـن بعـده، وكأنـه حي بينهـم متى ما تصفّح أحـدّ نصاً يحمل اسـم مُنشئه.

وجـاءت الشبكة العنكبوتيـة لتكثّـف فكرة التواصل وتسهّلها وتسرّعها. وكانـت اختراعاً هائلاً فـي مطلـع حدوثه، وصنـع الإنترنـت حدثاً ثقافياً وعلمياً لافتاً، إضافة إلى كونه حدثاً اقتصادياً خطيراً غيّر قواعد الاقتصاد ونظامه الفكري والتخطيطي، وكذلك أثر سياسيّاً وأمنياً، بحيث أصبحت السياسة نفسـها خطابـاً افتراضيـاً عبر تغيّـر نظامَـي التعبير والتفكيـر لتصبـغ صياغـة القول متسقة مـع أنواع لا تحصى مـن الاسـتقبالات. ولـم يعد الخطـاب موجهـاً إلـى طبقة واحـدة، وإنما أصبـح مفتوحاً لكل من تصله الرسـالة. وقـد انعكس هذا على حال الصياغـة عبـر الوعي بـأن ما يقال سـيصل وصولاً عالمياً وسـيبقى أيضً آ التاريـخ بالصوت والصورة ولغـة الجسـد، وهـي كلها صيغ مصاحبـة لصيغة النـص المكتوب الذي سـيصبح منطوقاً ومشـاهداً بـكل مصاحباته، وهذه الصيغ المتداخلة أفضت إلى صناعة لغة غير اللغة التقليديـة، ولها بلاغاتها الخاصة وأسـاليبها المختلفـة جذرياً.

وجـاءت مـع ذلك الانتشـار الهائـل مشكلة (الاختراق)، وهي أخطر مشـكلة تواجه البشـر حيث تحولت فكرة الحروب من مجرد أسلحة فتاكة تقتل إلى أسلحة خفية تدمر، من دون أن يكتشفها أحد إلا بعد حدوث التدمير، كأن يكتشـف أحدنا أن حسـابه البنكي يتناقص بسـرعة خاطفة أو تكتشـف شـركة مـا أن مخترِعها الذي تعمـل عليه وبسـرية مطلقة قـد تمت سـرقته عبـر حركة بسـيطة لكنها مهولة. وهذه حالٌ غيرت قواعـد الأمـن والأمـان وقواعد الخصوصية والسرية.

وكل نافـع هو ضار في الوقت ذاته وبالحتمية ذاتها. وهذا مـا حـرك نظريـات التحصـين الذاتـي وكيـف نحمي أنفسـنا، في حين نظل علـى تواصل مع العالم. وما بين رغبتنا في الحصول على خدمات سـريعة ومريحة وبين خوفنـا من سـرقة معلوماتنا

behavior. We desire, so we advance; we fear, so we halt. Our desires take control, but these feelings beget regret and elicit dread.

The Internet has remained a wellspring of these closely correlated states, especially considering the plethora of warnings issued by information-security agencies about the ploys of hackers. Here, we may add the notion of "information security" to our cultural balance, as something akin to personal security or the ownership of guard dogs tasked with alerting us to impending danger. We have long trusted dogs to guard us in our sleep, relying on their alertness and their barking to wake us in case of imminent danger. Despite these alerts, people still falter and remain stuck between their need for the Internet and their fear of it. Though human experience has shown that science prevails and imposes its presence through a system of practical and economic benefits, every gain is necessarily subject to losses. This formula leads humanity forward, between the options of desire and dread, a cost-benefit calculus, and an assessment as to which of the two is more significant. Human beings are, after all, inherently inclined to adventure, even at the risk of setbacks, such as the one suffered by Abbas ibn Firnas, who paid with his life for his desire and ambition. Still, the results of every adventure provide experience and help us to hone the scales of expectation. Despite his death, ibn Firnas presented humanity with a lesson to avoid his missteps. The Internet has therefore spurred our deep-seated desires, unleashing them to absolute freedom. Human freedom, the most significant of unquantifiable gains, lies in the choices made directly by human beings. This is the Internet's achievement, as it has made our choices absolute, without an overseer or mediator.

تظـل حياتنـا معلقةٌ بيــن رغبـة ورهبة. وكلمـا رهبنا جـاءت رغبـات السـرعة لتغرينا بالعـودة إلـى ما كنا خائفيــن منه.

هـذه حـال مباشـرة ويوميـة جعلنـا الإنترنت نعيشـها ونتقبلها بالضرورة الواقعية، وأخطر شـيء فيهـا هـو اكتشـافنا أن ذكاءنا الفطريّ غيـر قادر على حمايتنـا، فاحتجنا إلـى اختراع (الـذكاء الاصطناعي) ليسـاعدنا على مواجهة مشـاكل تقـدم التكنولوجيا، وهـذا الـذكاء الاصطناعـي أصبح أيضاً يهـدد أماننا وثقتنا بمقـدار ما يخدمنا، والحكمـة التي كنا نتحلى بها ما لبثـت أن أثبتـت أنها حماقة وتهـور، ويحدث هـذا بشـكل مباشـر كلما وقـع أحدنـا ضحيـةً للعبة احتيال تأتي عبر (الواتس اب)، وبمجرد ضغطة على رابط نراه بريئاً وسليماً، لكننا نقع فيه فتتحول الحال إلى حسـرة حارقـة، وقد كنا نظنهـا متعةً مسليةً ومفيـدة معاً.

هنا يتكشـف الضعـف البشـري والهشاشـة المعنوية التي نقع فيها بين تضارب حالتين نعيشهما دوماً وتقودان سـلوكنا دوماً وهما (الرغبة / والرهبة). فنحـن نرغب فنقـدم، ونهـاب فنتوقف، ولكـن الذي يحدث هو أن الرغبات هـي التي تتحكم، ولكنه تحكّم يـورث الندم ويسـتدعي الرهبة.

غيـر أن الإنترنت ظـل مصدراً لهاتيـن الحالتين في تلازم وثيـق، خاصة مـع كثـرة التنبيهـات من أجهـزة الأمـن المعلوماتي حـول حيـل المخترقين. وهنا نضيـف إلـى رصيدنـا الثقافي نظريـة (الأمن المعلوماتـي) لتكون مثل الأمن الذاتـي ومثل تملك كلاب الحراسـة التي تسـاعد علـى التنبيـه من خطر مقبل، وكان الإنسـان يثق بكلابه التي تحرسـه وقت منامـه ويعتمـد علـى نباهتها كـي توقظـه بصوتها ليحتـاط من خطر يلوح في الأفق. غير أن الإنسـان نفسـه يقع رغم التنبيهـات ويظل بيـن حاجتـه إلـى الإنترنـت ومخاوفه منها، ولكن العلـم ينتصر لنفسه كما تشـير تجارب البشـرية ويفرض وجوده عبـر منظومـة فوائـده العمليـة والاقتصادية وكل ربح هو بالضـرورة معرّض للخسـارة، وهذه معادلة

does the killing to one in which invisible weapons are only detected after they have wrought their destruction. It is akin to one realizing that their bank account balance is being rapidly depleted, or like when a company discovers that the invention it has been developing in absolute secrecy was stolen in one simple yet devastating swoop. This situation has altered the rules of safety, security, privacy, and secrecy.

Every benefit carries with it concurrent and inevitable harm. This has spurred notions of self-fortification and methods to protect ourselves while remaining connected to the world. Amid our wish for fast, convenient services and our fear of personal-information theft, our lives remain suspended between desire and dread. Whenever we experience that dread, our desire for speed lures us back toward that which we feared.

The Internet has led us to experience this state and to accept it as a daily imperative of reality. Most dangerous therein is our realization that our inborn intelligence is incapable of protecting us; this knowledge necessitated our invention of "artificial intelligence" as a means of helping people to face the challenges of technological advancement. This artificial intelligence has also come to threaten our sense of security and trust in what serves us and in the wisdom we possess, which soon proved to be foolishness and imprudence. We experience this every time we fall victim to a scam on WhatsApp, when—with a simple tap on a seemingly innocent and secure link—we find instant, bitter regret where we thought there would be entertainment and benefit in equal measure.

Human weakness and emotional fragility are exposed in the contradictions of our perpetual experience of desire and dread, both of which dictate our

تجعل البشرية تمضي بيـن خياري الرغبة والرهبة، ومن ثم قياس المكاسـب أمام الخسـائر، وأيهما أكثر ضرورة للإنسان، على أن للإنسان طبيعةً أصيلةً مع المغامرة حتى لو تعرّض لبعض الانتكاسات وبعض المخاطـر كمثـال تجربـة عبـاس بـن فرنـاس التـي جعلتـه يدفـع بحياتـه من أجـل رغبتـه ومطمحه، ورغـم موته فقد قـدم درسـاً للبشـرية تعلمت منه تجنـب نواقـص تجربة ابـن فرنـاس، وكل مغامـرة تعطـي نتائجها خبرة مـن جهة وتحسـيناً لدرجات التوقع من جهة ثانيـة. وهنا نقول إن الإنترنت حفّز فينـا الرغبـات العميقـة وأطلقتها بحرية مطلقة، وحرية الإنسان دومـاً هي فـي خياراته التـي تتصل به مباشرةً وهي المكسـب المعنوي الأهم، وهذا ما حققه الإنترنت من حيـث إنه جعل خياراتنا مطلقةً مـن دون رقيب ومن دون وسـيط.

مقابلــــة مع الفنانــــة
د. إيمــــان الجبريــــن
INTERVIEW WITH THE ARTIST
DR EIMAN ELGIBREEN

آرام العجاجي
Aram Alajaji

In advance of *The Silent Age of Singularity*, Misk Art Institute Assistant Curator, Aram Alajaji, interviewed Dr. Eiman Elgibreen, a distinguished artist and art historian, about her experiences during the transformative post-Internet era of Saudi Arabia's cultural landscape. Elgibreen's journey through the digital age reflects the evolving dynamics between tradition and innovation in the context of contemporary art. One of the early adopters of the Internet in the late 1990s, she recounts how this digital revolution both inspired her practice and transformed her approach to art, granting her access to global resources and tools that were previously unavailable on the local market. She also highlights the Internet's role in fostering community among Saudi artists, which has allowed them to connect, collaborate, and explore new mediums despite the lack of local art institutions. Elgibreen's experiences underscore the significant impact of the Internet on the development of contemporary art.

عنـد انطلاقـة سلسـلة الأعمـال التحضيريـة لمعرض «عصر الأثر الخافت»، أجرت القيّمة الفنية المساعدة في معهد مسـك للفنـون آرام العجاجي، مقابلة مع الفنانـة والمؤرخـة الفنيـة الدكتـورة إيمـان الجبرين؛ تحدثـت فيهـا عـن تجاربهـا خـلال الحقبـة التحولية في المشـهد الثقافي السعودي بعد ظهور الإنترنت، وتعكس رحلتهـا الديناميكيـات المتغيّـرة بين التقليد والابتـكار في سـياق الفـن المعاصر، وتُعـد من أوائل مَن تبنوا الإنترنـت في أواخر التسـعينيات من القرن الماضي. وتروي هنا كيف شـكّلت هذه الثورة الرقمية مصدر إلهام لها في ممارسـتها الفنيـة، وكيف غيرت في الوقـت ذاته مقاربتهـا للفن عبر إتاحتهـا إمكانية الوصـول إلى المـوارد والأدوات العالمية التي لم تكن متوفرة فـي السـوق المحلية. كمـا تسـلّط الجبرين الضوء من خلال المقابلة على دور الإنترنت في تعزيز الشـعور بالانتماء الجماعي بين الفنانين السعوديين، ما مكّنهم من التواصل والتعاون واستكشاف الوسائل الجديدة رغم محدودية المؤسسات الفنية المحلية. وتؤكـد تجـارب الجبريـن علـى التأثيـر العميـق الذي أحدثه الإنترنت في مسـيرة تطور الفـن المعاصر.

harsh attack on Arabs and Muslims after 9/11. This unsecured exposure to what "others" thought of us traumatized me for many years, and it became the focal point of all of my early work, inspiring me to ask questions about stereotypes. My later work is a developed stage of that trauma, as it attempts to reconcile with the human inability to escape the mind's eye. Our preconceptions control our vision, and it is extremely difficult to avoid that.

EE: The Internet era was a pivotal time for the arts in Saudi Arabia, and it fostered a sense of community among artists that was previously unheard of. It revolutionized our industry, providing a visual wealth of inspiration and compensating for the lack of art museums in the country. It gave artists access to tools and mediums they were eager to try, but were unavailable on the local market. It also opened the doors to international art competitions, workshops, educational resources, and communities. I remember in 2003, a substantial Saudi art group was created on Yahoo; it became our first source of art news. There was also an art forum called Al-Marsam, and it became our community's largest and most important platform. It's not an exaggeration to say that even the most junior members of the forum back then have become leading figures in the Saudi art scene today. We always laugh together when we randomly discover that we were pen pals through that forum, and we tease each other to find out the other's pseudonyms.

سـؤال: دكتـورة إيمـان، لقد عايشـت حقبـة ما بعد الإنترنت عن كثب ولم تقتصري على ذلك، بل تفاعلت معهـا بقوة كفنانـة، ومعلوم أن ظهـور الإنترنت في التسعينيات من القرن العشرين شكل تحولاً كبيراً في كيفية تفاعلنا وتواصلنا وإبداعنـا، هل يمكنك وصف هذه الحقبة من منظورك الشخصي ومشاركة أفكارك حـول تأثيـر دخـول الإنترنت علـى المشـهد الثقافي، وبخاصة في المملكة العربية السـعودية؟

جـواب: حالفنـي الحـظ فكنـت واحـدة مـن أوائـل الأشخاص الذين استخدموا الإنترنت نظراً لأن أشقائي الأكبر سـنّاً وصلوا إلـى الإنترنت في عملهـم منذ عام 1996 قبـل أن يكـون متاحـاً للجمهـور، كنـت حينها لا أزال في الخامسـة عشـرة مـن عمـري، لكنني كنت مصممـة علـى متابعة شـغفي بالفن، ولهـذا بدأت في انتقاء كتب الفن وشـراء الكثير منها عبر الإنترنت لأننـي لم أكـن راغبة فـي الاقتصار على ما هـو متاح في السـوق السـعودي، ولم أرغب بالإلحاح في طلب جلبها من الأشـخاص المسـافرين إلى الخـارج، وقد حماني هذا الاسـتخدام المهني المبكـر للإنترنت من الوقوع في فـخ الانغماس في غرف الدردشة عندما أصبـح الإنترنت متاحـاً للجمهور في عـام 1999. في ذلك العام، بدأتُ أيضاً دراستي الجامعية في الرياض، فصـار لدي مبرر لطلب لـوازم الفن مـن جميع أنحاء العالـم، والتي نزلـت حديثاً إلى الأسـواق الدولية، كما صـار بإمكانـي الاشـتراك فـي العديـد مـن المجلّات الفنيـة، ما سـاعدني في توطيـد معارفـي ومهاراتي، وفي تشكيل أسلوبي الفني قبل أقراني. والمهمة الأكثر تحديـاً آنذاك كانت في إقناع الشـركات عبـر الإنترنت بشـحن البضائـع إلى السـعودية، ففـي تلـك الفترة، لم يكـن بلدنا مدرجاً فـي قائمة البلـدان على معظم المواقـع الإلكترونيـة، وكان هناك خوف مـن الحرب البيولوجيـة بعد أحـداث 11 سـبتمبر، ما أثّر للأسـف علـى الأعمال التجاريـة. ومع ذلك، تمكنتُ من إقناع معظـم المواقـع الإلكترونية بشـحن المنتجات لي.

أحد الجوانب المؤلمة في عصر ما بعد الإنترنت هو أننا تعرّضنا في سن المراهقة للهجوم القاسي على العرب والمسلمين بعد أحداث 11 سبتمبر، وقد تسبّب

 Dr. Eiman, you have not only experienced the post-Internet era firsthand, but also actively engaged with it as an artist. The introduction of the Internet in the 1990s marked a significant shift in how we interact, communicate, and create. Could you describe this era from your perspective and share your thoughts on how the entrance of the Internet transformed the cultural landscape, particularly in Saudi Arabia?

Eiman Elgibreen (EE): I was lucky to be one of the very first people to use the Internet because my older siblings had access to it through their jobs beginning in 1996, before it really became accessible to the public. I was still fifteen, but I was already determined to follow my passion for art. Therefore, I started to choose art books for myself and order many of them online. I didn't want to be limited to what was available on the Saudi market or have to ask someone to get me books when they traveled. This early professional introduction to the Internet protected me from falling into the trap of chat rooms, when the Internet was finally available to the masses in 1999. That was also the year I started university in Riyadh. Therefore, I had an excuse to order art supplies, to experiment with, from around the world that had been newly introduced to the international market. I could also subscribe to many art magazines, which advanced my knowledge and skills, and they helped me to shape my style sooner than my peers. The most challenging task back then was to convince online companies to ship to Saudi Arabia. Our country was not listed in the country list on most early websites, and there was a fear of biological warfare after 9/11 which unfortunately affected the trade business. However, I managed to convince most of them to ship to me.

One traumatizing aspect of the post-Internet era is that we were brutally exposed as teens to the

هذا التعرّض غير المحمي لما كان يعتقده "الآخرون"، في إحداث صدمة لي لسنوات عديدة، وأصبحت هذه الصدمة النقطة المحورية في جميع أعمالي المبكرة، ودفعتني إلى طرح الأسئلة حول الصور النمطية؛ أما عن أعمالي اللاحقة فتمثل مرحلة متطورة من هذه الصدمة، حيث حاولتُ التصالح مع عجز الإنسان عن الهروب من عين العقل، وإن تصوراتنا المسبقة تتحكّم برؤيتنا؛ ومن الصعب للغاية تجنّب ذلك.

جواب: شكّل عصر الإنترنت فترةً محورية للفنون في المملكة العربية السـعودية، وعزّز الشـعور بالجماعة بيـن الفنانيـن أكثـر مـن ذي قبـل، وأحدث ثـورة في القطـاع الفني، ووفّر مصـادر بصرية هائلـة، معوّضاً بذلك نقـص المتاحـف الفنية فـي البلاد؛ لقـد أتاح عصر الإنترنت للفنانيـن إمكانية الوصول إلى الأدوات والوسائط التي كانوا يتعطّشون لتجربتها، ولكنها لم تكـن متاحة فـي السـوق المحلية، كما فتـح الأبواب أمام المشـاركة في المسـابقات الفنية وورش العمل والوصـول إلـى المـوارد التعليميـة والتواصـل مـع الأوسـاط الفنية على المستوى الدولي، ولا أزال أتذكّر تلك المجموعة الفنية السعودية الكبيرة التي أنشئت على موقع "ياهو" في عام 2003 وأصبحت مصدرنا الأول لأخبار الفن، كان هنالك أيضاً منتدى فني باسـم "المرسـم"، أصبح أكبر وأهم منصة للفنانين السـعوديين. وليـس مـن المبالغـة القـول إن حتى أصغـر أعضاء المنتـدى في ذلك الوقت قد أصبحوا فـي يومنا هذا شـخصيات رائدة في المشـهد الفني السـعودي، ولا نـزال نضحـك اليوم عندما نكتشـف بالصدفة أننا كنا أصدقاء مراسـلة على ذلك المنتدى،

their initial reactions are when I first meet them, depending on their preconceptions of my gender, race, and choice of dress.

As for the post-Internet era, I had no artistic career in the 1990s. Therefore, I would not say that the Internet led to a shift in my career. Rather, it "shaped" my artistic style and expression to the max since I started learning art during the introductory era of the Internet. As I already explained, the Internet not only gave me access to endless art styles, mediums, tools, and sources of inspiration, but it also made me confront many issues that I would have never thought about if I hadn't had this limitless access to the rest of the world. It helped me to see myself and my culture through a different lens and start questioning everything I believed in.

EE: Yes, for sure. Audiences and professionals alike were nice enough to teach me valuable information and give me insight into the art world. For example, in 2002, I was twenty-one years old, and no one around me knew how to access art biennials. Therefore, I started contacting people who work in different

ونستهزئ بأسمائنا المستعارة آنذاك؛ لقد استطعنا التعبير عن أنفسنا بحرية وقلنا أشياء ربما لم نكن لنتحلى بالشجاعة الكافية لقولها بصوتٍ عالٍ في ذلك الوقت، وبخاصة في حكمنا على أعمال فنانين آخرين. إنه تاريخ لا يفهمه ويقدّره سوى من عاشه. وبهذا ندرك أهمية مثل تلك المنصات البسيطة.

وكان للإنترنت أثرٌ بالغ الأهمية في إثراء التنوع في الفن السعودي، لا سيما في مجالات الوسائط الرقمية والأساليب غير التقليدية، وأتاح هذا التحول للعديد من المبدعين تحقيق أحلامهم في أن يصبحوا فنانين، بغض النظر عن مؤهلاتهم الأكاديمية أو افتقارهم لها، ولا يكمن تأثير الإنترنت في تمكين الانتفاع منه فحسب، بل أيضاً في طابعه المفتوح للجميع، ما سمح بظهور مجموعة واسعة من أشكال التعبير الفني في المشهد الفني السعودي. وهذا التنوع هو ما أضفى على الساحة الفنية مزيداً من الحيوية والتشويق أكثر من أي وقت مضى.

وعلى وجه العموم، يتميّز السعوديون بحبهم للمغامرة واستكشاف كل ما هو جديد؛ وهذا أمر متجذّر متأصّل فيهم باعتبارهم أحفاد الرحّل الذين جابوا الصحراء. ولذلك كان من الطبيعي أن يؤثر دخول الإنترنت تأثيراً بالغاً على ثقافتنا.

جواب: لا تركّز سلسلة "الأقنعة الإلكترونية" بالضرورة على الجانب السلبي للاتصال الرقمي، فردود الفعل السلبية حدثت فقط عندما التقيتُ بالطرف الآخر المعني شخصياً. ولهذا السبب، حرصت على إرفاق نسخة من المراسلات الإلكترونية التي جرت قبل الاجتماع الأول، وهدفي هنا أن يقرأ الجمهور مدى

We expressed ourselves freely and said things that we may never have been brave enough to say out loud back then, especially when we judged other artists' work. It's a history that only those who lived through can truly appreciate; we understand the importance of such a simple platform.

Another significant influence of the Internet was promoting diversity in Saudi art, particularly in digital mediums and nontraditional styles. This shift allowed many creative individuals to pursue their dreams of becoming artists, regardless of their academic training or lack thereof. The Internet's influence was not just about access, but about inclusivity: it opened the doors for a diverse range of artistic expressions in the Saudi art scene. This diversity that has enriched our art scene and made it more vibrant and exciting than ever before.

Saudis are generally adventurous and love to explore new things. This is embedded in their DNA as descendants of the migrants of the desert. Therefore, it was expected that the introduction of the Internet would significantly impact our culture.

EE: *Electronic Veils* does not necessarily highlight a negative aspect of digital communication. Adverse reactions only happen when I meet with the other party involved in person. This is why I intentionally attach a copy of the email correspondence that came before the first meeting. I want the audience to read how endearing the text is throughout the emails written by different individuals—and how different

جاذبية النصوص في تلك الرسـائل، وكيف اختلفت ردود أفعـال الأشـخاص الذيـن كتبوهـا عنـد لقائي الأول بهم بناءً على تصوراتهم المسـبقة عن جنسي وعرقي وهيئتي.

في مـا يتعلق بعصر مـا بعد الإنترنـت، لم أكن قـد بدأت مسـيرتي الفنية بعد في تسـعينيات القرن الماضـي. لـذا، لا يمكنني القـول إن الإنترنـت أدى إلى تحـول في أسـلوبي الفنـي؛ بل بالأحـرى، إنه "صاغ" بالكامل أسـلوبي وتوجهاتي الفنيـة منذ بداية تعلمي الفن في مستهلّ عصر الإنترنت، وكما أوضحتُ سابقاً، لم يمنحني الإنترنت فقط القدرة على الوصول إلى ما لا يُعد ولا يُحصى من الأسـاليب والوسـائط والأدوات ومصادر الإلهـام الفنية، بل قادني أيضاً إلى التعامل مـع العديد من القضايـا التي لم أكـن لأفكـر فيها لولا هـذا الوصول غير المحدود إلى العالم؛ لقد سـاعدني في رؤية نفسـي وثقافتي من خلال عدسـة مختلفة، ودفعني إلى التسـاؤل حول كل ما كنـت أؤمن به.

سـؤال: مع تطور الإنترنت، شـهدنا توسعاً هائلاً في التواصل العالمـي، وأدى ازدهـار المدوّنات ومنصات الرسـائل في وضع الأسـس لمـا أصبح لاحقـاً التأثير الأكبر لوسـائل التواصل الاجتماعي. فاليوم، تغلغلت المنصات الرقمية مثل فايسبوك وانسـتغرام وإكس تغلغلاً عميقاً في جميـع جوانب حياتنا تقريباً، حيث تربط هـذه المنصـات بين مليـارات الأشـخاص من جميـع أرجـاء العالم. وتسـتغلها الشـركات الإعلانية العالمية إلى أقصى حد، وتسـتفيد منها الشخصيات العامة في رسـم مسيرتها وتشـكيل صورتها. في ظل هذا المشهد الرقمي المتسارع، كيف أثّر الإنترنت على طريقة تقديمك لأعمالـك الفنية؟ وهل غيّر الإنترنت ووسائل التواصل الاجتماعي من نهجك في الوصول إلى جمهورك والتفاعل مع الأوساط الفنية العالمية؟

جـواب: نعـم، بالتأكيـد. لقـد كان الجمهـور والمحترفون كرماء بما يكفي ليزوّدوني بالمعلومات القيّمـة ويمنحوني رؤيـة ثاقبة لعالم الفـن، على سـبيل المثال، في عـام 2002، كنت فـي الحادية والعشـرين مـن عمـري، ولم يكن أحد ممـن حولي

museums and art organizations and had online profiles. There were only a few of them. However, one person from Germany was generous enough to respond and explain the different methods of showing your work in a biennial. I had numerous incidents that helped me immensely to set realistic approaches to reach my goals. These people and their acts of kindness helped me to become who I am today.

Thanks to communicating through the Internet, I could take my work to places far away, worldwide, without an agent or a gallery.

EE: To be honest, I do not recall any challenges related to the Internet, other than the expensive service fees when it was first introduced. And the training required to master all the tools and programs related to it. However, I believe I am privileged to have had very supportive and well-informed family members who provided all of that to help me adapt quickly.

يعـرف كيفيـة الوصـول إلـى بيناليـات الفنـون. لذا، تواصلـت مـع أشـخاص يعملـون فـي مختلـف المتاحـف والمنظمات الفنية، وكان لديهم حسـابات علـى الإنترنـت – وكان عددهم قليلاً آنـذاك. غير أن شـخصاً من ألمانيـا تلطّف بالرد وشـرح لـي الطرق المختلفـة لعـرض أعمالـي فـي البيناليـات، ومررتُ بالعديـد من المواقـف التي سـاعدتني بشـكل كبير علـى وضع اسـتراتيجيات واقعيـة لتحقيق أهدافي، هؤلاء الأشـخاص وأفعالهـم الكريمـة، كان لهم دور كبيـر فـي أن أصبح الشـخص الـذي أنا عليـه اليوم.

فضلاً عن ذلك، وبفضل التواصل عبر الإنترنت، تمكّنـتُ من إيصـال أعمالي إلى أماكـن بعيدة حول العالـم دون الحاجة إلى وكيل أو غاليري.

سـؤال: يجلب كل عصر معه تحديات وفرصاً فريدة، فبصفتـك فنانة تعملين في عصر مـا بعد الإنترنت، ما هي التحديات التي واجهتـك؟ أو ما هي الفرص التي أتاحهـا لك هذا العصر؟

جـواب: بصراحـة، لا أتذكر أي تحديـات مرتبطـة بالإنترنت، عدا رسـوم الخدمة الباهظة في البداية، والتدريب المطلوب لإتقان جميع الأدوات والبرامج ذات الصلة. وأعتقـد أننـي كنت محظوظـة لكوني محاطـة بأسـرة داعمـة ومطّلعة قدمت لـي كل ما أحتاجـه، ما سـاعدني على التكيف بسرعة.

الفنانون وأعمالهم

ARTISTS
& ARTWORKS

إبراهيــم أبـو مسمار
IBRAHIM ABUMSMAR
p. 30 .ص

مهــدي الجريبــي
MAHDI ALJERAIBI
p. 36 .ص

تركــي القحطانــي
TURKI ALQAHTANI
p. 40 .ص

عمــر الزهرانــي
OMAR ALZAHRANI
p. 44 .ص

محمــد شـــرورو
MOHAMMED CHROURO
p. 48 .ص

أيمــن يسري ديدبــان
AYMAN YOSSRI DAYDBAN
p. 56 .ص

إيمــان الجبريــن
EIMAN ELGIBREEN
p. 60 .ص

منيــر فاطمــي
MOUNIR FATMI
p. 70 .ص

ســعيد قمحـاوي
SAEED GAMHAWI
p. 76 .ص

ســامية حلبــي
SAMIA HALABY
p. 80 .ص

ديفيـــد هوكنـــي
DAVID HOCKNEY
ص. p. 90

ســـفيان الإدريســي
SOUFIANE IDRISSI
ص. p. 98

زيـــاد كحكــــي
ZIAD KAKI
ص. p. 108

خالـــــد مخشـــــوش
KHALED MAKHSHOUSH
ص. p. 112

أحمــــد ماطــــر
AHMED MATER
ص. p. 118

بينيـــــت ميلـــــر
BENNETT MILLER
ص. p. 122

نـــام جـــون بايـــك
NAM JUNE PAIK
ص. p. 130

جـــــون سالفيســـــت
JOHN SALVEST
ص. p. 142

فيصـــــل ســـــمرة
FAISAL SAMRA
ص. p. 146

آنيـــا ســـليمان
ANIA SOLIMAN
ص. p. 152

إبراهيم أبو مسمار

(مواليد 1976،
المملكة العربية السعودية)
يقيم ويعمل في أبها
(المملكة العربية السعودية)

إبراهيم أبو مسمار هو فنانٌ متعدد التخصصات، دفعه شغفه بالفن والتصوير الفوتوغرافي إلى متابعة دورات أكاديمية في الرسم الزيتي والبورتريه والتصميم والنحت والتصوير الفوتوغرافي والخط العربي والديكور في وكالة الغوري للفنون التراثية في القاهرة، مصر، ودرس لاحقاً الفنون الجميلة بجامعة حلوان في القاهرة، وتتمحور مزاولته الفنية حول النظر في جوهر الأشياء اليومية وهويتها، فالمنحوتات التي يبتدعها لأسباب رمزية أكثر من كونها عملية تتحدى التطبيق العملي المحسوس للأشياء المصنعة - وهي فكرة لها تأثير وجداني لا واعٍ على الحياة اليومية.

شارك في العديد من المعارض الجماعية، سواءً على المستوى المحلي أو الدولي، ومن أبرزها "الجو: سردية الأشياء" في غاليري دي بالقاهرة، مصر (2023)؛ آرت أبوظبي مع غاليري أثر بأبوظبي، الإمارات العربية المتحدة (2022)؛ و"خارج المألوف" في غاليري أثر بجدة، المملكة العربية السعودية (2019)؛ والنسخة الخامسة من فن جدة 21,39 في المجلس الفني السعودي، المملكة العربية السعودية (2018)؛ و"من الصحراء إلى الدلتا: الفن المعاصر في ممفيس" في جامعة ممفيس، الولايات المتحدة الأمريكية (2017)؛ ومتحف "الصندوق الأخضر" للفن السعودي المعاصر بأمستردام، هولندا (2015)؛ و"مدارات 6" لومولان في غاليري كونتينوا بباريس، فرنسا (2013)؛ آرت دبي مع غاليري أثر بأبوظبي، الإمارات العربية المتحدة (2012)؛ و"نحن بحاجة إلى التحدث"، حافة الجزيرة العربية بجدة، المملكة العربية السعودية (2012)؛ غاليري أثر في مهرجان

الفنون في مراكش (2011)؛ و"النماء والعطاء" بخميس مشيط، المملكة العربية السعودية (2011)؛ و"مراسم الأمل" بجدة، المملكة العربية السعودية (2010)؛ و"معرض جائزة أبها الثقافية"، أبها، المملكة العربية السعودية (2009)؛ و"معرض جمعية الثقافة والفنون" بعسير مول، عسير، المملكة العربية السعودية (2009)؛ و"معرض القوات المسلحة"، المنطقة الجنوبية، المملكة العربية السعودية (2007).

IBRAHIM ABUMSMAR

(b. 1976, Saudi Arabia)
Lives and works in Abha,
Saudi Arabia

Ibrahim Abumsmar is a multidisciplinary artist whose passion for art and photography led him to pursue academic courses in oil painting, portraiture, design, sculpture, photography, Arabic calligraphy, and interior architecture at Beit Al-Ghouri in Cairo, Egypt. He later studied fine art at Helwan University in Cairo. The artist's practice often centers on questioning the essence and identity of everyday objects: his sculptures challenge the perceived practicality of manufactured objects, suggesting that they were created for more symbolic than practical reasons—an idea that impacts our lives on a subconscious, emotional level.

Abumsmar has participated in numerous group exhibitions, both locally and internationally. Notable exhibitions include *Atmospheric: Objects of Narrative*, Art D, Cairo, Egypt (2023); Art Abu Dhabi with Athr Gallery, Abu Dhabi, UAE (2022); *Out of Place*, Athr Gallery, Jeddah, Saudi Arabia (2019); the 5th edition of 21, 39 Jeddah Arts, Saudi Art Council, Saudi Arabia (2018); *Desert to Delta: Contemporary Art in Memphis*, University of Memphis, USA (2017); Greenbox Museum of Contemporary Art from Saudi Arabia, Amsterdam, The Netherlands (2015); *SPHERES 6*, Le Moulin, Galleria Continua, Paris, France (2013); Art Dubai with Athr Gallery, Abu Dhabi, UAE (2012); *We Need to Talk*, Edge of Arabia, Jeddah, Saudi Arabia (2012); Athr Gallery at the Marrakech Art Fair, Morocco (2011); *Al-Nama' and Al-Atta'*, Khamees Musheet, Saudi Arabia (2011); *Marasim Al-A'amal*, Jeddah, Saudi Arabia (2010); the *Abha Cultural Award* exhibition, Abha, Saudi Arabia (2009); *Society of Arts and Culture Exhibition*, Aseer Mall, Aseer, Saudi Arabia (2009); and *The Armed Forces Exhibition*, Southern Province, Saudi Arabia (2007).

إبراهيم أبو مسمار
(مواليد 1976، المملكة العربية السعودية)

لا توجد إشارة، 2006

فلم قصير
3 دقائق و57 ثانية
بإذن من الفنان

إبراهيم أبو مسمار
(مواليد 1976، المملكة العربية السعودية)

لا توجد إشارة، 2006

ورق فابريانو
130 × 80 سم
بإذن من الفنان

NO SIGNAL

لا توجد إشارة

IBRAHIM ABUMSMAR
(b. 1976, Saudi Arabia)

No Signal, 2015

Short film
3 min., 57 sec.
Courtesy of the artist

إبراهيـــم أبو مســـمار
(مواليد 1976، المملكة العربية السعودية)

لا توجد إشارة، 2015

فلم قصير
3 دقائق و57 ثانية
بإذن من الفنان

IBRAHIM ABUMSMAR
(b. 1976, Saudi Arabia)

No Signal, 2015

Fabriano paper
130 × 80 cm
Courtesy of the artist

إبراهيـــم أبو مســـمار
(مواليد 1976، المملكة العربية السعودية)

لا توجد إشارة، 2015

ورق فابريانو
130 × 80 سم
بإذن من الفنان

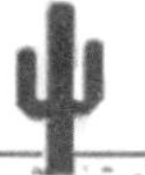

الاتصال بالإنترنت مقطوع

يمكنك محاولة:
- التحقق من كابلات الشبكة، والمودم، وجهاز التوجيه
- إعادة الاتصال بـ Wi-Fi

ERR_INTERNET_DISCONNECTED

مهــــدي الجريبــــي

(مواليد 1969،
المملكة العربية السعودية)
يقيم ويعمل في مكة المكرمة
(المملكة العربية السعودية)

مهدي الجريبي هو فنانٌ تجريدي سريالي متعدد الوسائط، يستكشف في أعماله مختلف الموضوعات المرتبطة بالثقافة، مستحضراً فكرة الذاكرة الجماعية، تخرّج من معهد التربية الفنية بالرياض عام 1989، ثم عمل مدرساً للفن في مكة المكرمة، ويدمج في مزاولته الفنية البحث المنهجي ويستخدم مجموعة متنوعة من الوسائط كالرسم والنحت والتركيب، حيث يتناول موضوعات الهوية والتقاليد والحداثة ويعيد إحياء القصص المخفية للأشياء الجاهزة التي يلتقط من خلالها التاريخ.

شارك الجريبي في العديد من المعارض الجماعية، من أبرزها؛ "مساحة مشتركة" في غاليري العالمية بجدة، المملكة العربية السعودية (2011)؛ و"حافة الجزيرة العربية" في قاعة بروناي بكلية الدراسات الشرقية والإفريقية في جامعة لندن، المملكة المتحدة (2008)؛ و"بابل" في سيول، كوريا الجنوبية (2002)؛ و"قوة الروح: 30 فناناً ضد مرض الزهايمر" في غاليري دروو مونتاني بباريس، فرنسا (2002)؛ بينالي القاهرة الدولي التاسع، مصر (2003)؛ و"الفن للجميع" في مؤسسة المنصورية بجدة، المملكة العربية السعودية (2000)؛ و"أعمال مختارة من الفن السعودي المعاصر"، إسبانيا (1989)؛ و"سرفانتيس"، المكسيك (1996). وتشمل معارضه الفردية "لهجات" في أتيليه جدة، المملكة العربية السعودية (2000)؛ المدينة الدولية للفنون بباريس، فرنسا (2000)؛ و"جدل" في أتيليه جدة المملكة العربية السعودية (1997).

دخلت أعماله إلى المجموعة الفنية لمؤسسة المنصورية في جدة بالمملكة العربية السعودية.

MAHDI ALJERAIBI

(b. 1969, Saudi Arabia)
Lives and works in Makkah,
Saudi Arabia

Mahdi Aljeraibi is a multimedia abstract surrealist artist who often explores themes relating to culture, thus evoking the idea of collective memory in his works. He graduated from the Institute of Art Education, Riyadh, in 1989, and then he worked as an art teacher in Makkah. The artist incorporates a process of systematic research and employs a variety of media, including painting, sculpture, and installation, as he addresses themes of identity, tradition, and modernity. He frequently brings to life the hidden stories of ready-made objects through which he captures history.

Aljeraibi has participated in numerous group exhibitions, including *Common Space*, Alalamia Gallery, Jeddah, Saudi Arabia (2011); *Edge of Arabia*, Brunei Gallery, SOAS University of London, UK (2008); *Babel*, Seoul, South Korea (2002); *La Force de l'Esprit: 30 Artistes contre la maladie d'Alzheimers*, Drouot Montaigne, Paris, France (2002); 9th Cairo International Biennale, Egypt (2003); *Art for All*, Al-Mansouria Foundation, Jeddah, Saudi Arabia (2000); *Selected Works of Saudi Contemporary Art Exhibition*, Spain (1989); and *Serphantis*, Mexico (1996). His solo exhibitions include *Dialects*, Jeddah Atelier, Saudi Arabia (2000); Cité internationale des arts, Paris, France (2000); and *Jadal*, Jeddah Atelier, Saudi Arabia (1997).

The artist's works can be found in the collection of the Al-Mansouria Foundation, Jeddah, Saudi Arabia.

مهــــدي الجريبــــي

(مواليد 1969، المملكة العربية السعودية)

جدل، *2000*

طاولة تلميذ/لوح خشبي

60 × 40 سم

بإذن من الفنان

ومؤسسة المنصورية في جدة

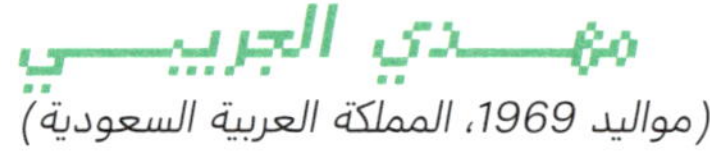

MAHDI ALJERAIBI

(b. 1969, Saudi Arabia)

Dialectic, 2000

Wooden desktops
40 × 60 cm each
Courtesy of the artist
and Al-Mansouria Foundation, Jeddah

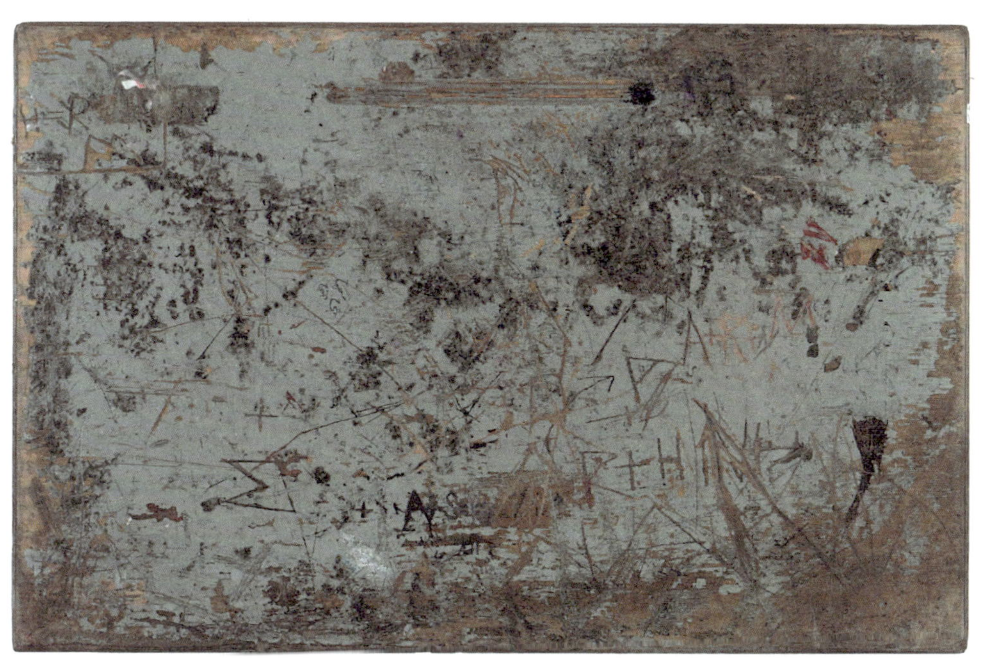

تركي القحطاني

(مواليد 2000،
المملكة العربية السعودية)
يقيم ويعمل في الرياض
(المملكة العربية السعودية)

تركي القحطاني فنانٌ إعلامي وصانع أفلام صاعد يصور الزخارف العربية مستكشفاً قضايا الهوية، والثقافة، والتقاليد، والحداثة، ومنذ تخرجه بدرجة الماجستير في التسويق الرقمي من كلية الملك بلندن في عام 2022، انكب على دمج رؤاه الإعلامية الرقمية في مزاولته الفنية، وهو يعمل حالياً في قسم التراث الرقمي في هيئة تطوير بوابة الدرعية، وشارك في معرض البحرين السنوي الخمسين للفنون التشكيلية في عام 2024. نشأ تركي في البحرين، وانجذب إلى الفن من خلال جولاته الوثائقية التي التقط خلالها جمال الأشياء العادية الذي نادراً ما يجذب الانتباه، وقد تطور انخراطه المبكر ببيئته إلى أسلوب متميز يجمع بين الإبداع المادي والرقمي.

في عام 2023، شارك القحطاني في إقامة فنية في معهد مسك للفنون، حيث قدم مشروعاً بحثياً حول الأصالة في الفن والذكاء الاصطناعي، كما تلقّى تدريباً على يد الفنان السعودي حمود العطاوي من خلال برنامج التوجيه والإرشاد بهيئة الفنون البصرية الذي تشرف عليه وزارة الثقافة في المملكة العربية السعودية.

TURKI ALQAHTANI

(b. 2000, Saudi Arabia)
Lives and works in Riyadh,
Saudi Arabia

Turki Alqahtani is an emerging media artist and film-maker who captures Arab motifs and often explores identity, culture, tradition, and modernity. Since graduating with an MSc in digital marketing from King's College London in 2022, the artist has been integrating his digital media insights with his artistic practice. Currently, Alqahtani works in digital heritage at the Diriyah Gate Development Authority, and he participated in the 50th Bahrain Annual Fine Arts Exhibition in 2024. Raised in Bahrain, he was drawn to art through documentary walks in which he captured the subtle, often overlooked, beauty of the ordinary. This early engagement with his environment evolved into a distinctive style that marries the tangible with digital creativity.

In 2023, Alqahtani took part in a residency at Misk Art Institute, where he presented a research project on authenticity in art and artificial intelligence. He was also mentored by Saudi Arabian artist Hmoud Alattawai through the Visual Arts Commission Mentorship & Guidance Program supervised by the Ministry of Culture, Saudi Arabia.

تركــــي القحطانــــي
(مواليد 2000، المملكة العربية السعودية)

كيلوبايت، 2024

تركيب فني باستخدام الفيديو
2160 × 3840 بكسل
1دقيقة، 12 ثانية حلقة
بإذن من الفنان

TURKI ALQAHTANI
(b. 2000, Saudi Arabia)

Kilobytes, 2024

Video installation
2160 × 3840 pixels
1 min., 12 sec. loop
Courtesy of the artist

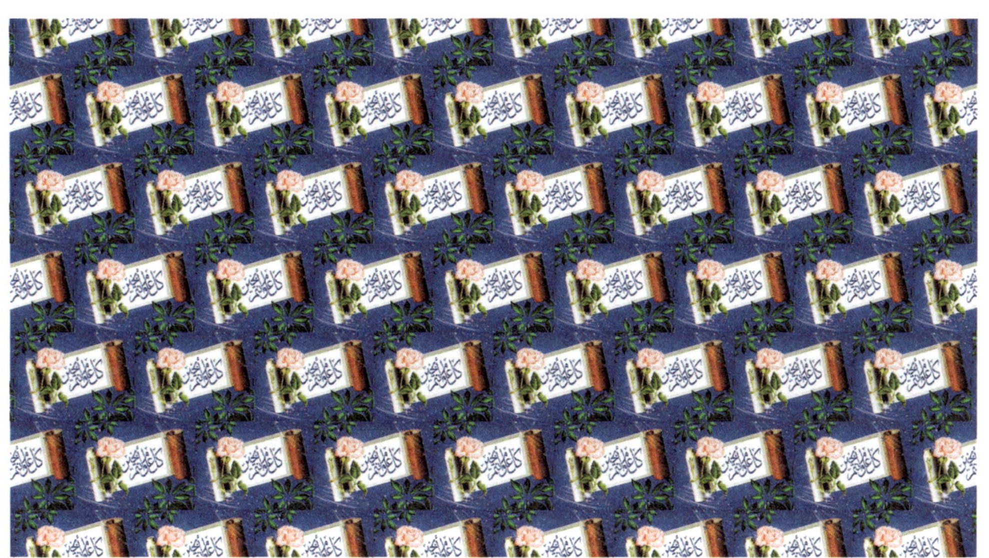

عمـــر الزهرانــي

(مواليد 1969،
المملكة العربية السعودية)
يقيم ويعمل في الرياض
(المملكة العربية السعودية)

عمـر الزهرانـي، المعـروف سـابقاً باسـم عـوض الزهرانـي، رسـامّ نشـأ وترعـرع فـي مكة، فُتـن بتنوع الناس الذيـن يؤمّون مدينته، مـا دفعه إلى محاولة تمثيل التأثيـرات التـي حملوهـا معهـم فـي فنـه؛ حصل على درجة الماجسـتير في التربية الفنية من جامعـة أم القـرى في مكة، وانغمس بعـد تخرجه فـي عالم الفنـون من خلال مشـاركته فـي عدد من الندوات والـدورات التدريبية التـي نظمتها مختلف المؤسسـات والهيئات، بما فيهـا أتيليـه جدة ومركز تسـامي للفنون البصرية، وتتضمن لوحاته التعبيرية التجريدية شحنةً عاطفية وجدانية عالية، من حيث إنه يسـتمد من الأصـوات والضوضـاء والروائـح التي تنبض بها مكـة متأثراً بالتجارب الحسـية المتنوعة فيهـا، كمـا يسـتحضر فـي أعماله لحظـات زمنيـة معينـة ويسـتخدم عمـق الألـوان وقـوام المـواد وضربـات الفرشـاة لالتقاط مـزاج تلـك المَشـاهد وأجوائها، ويخلـق مـن خـلال ضربـات الفرشـاة الديناميكيـة حركات واسـعة عبر لوحـات لا تقتصر علـى اتجـاه واحد، بـل تهدف إلى إثارة اسـتجابات وجدانيـة قوية لـدى الناظر.

شـارك فـي العديـد مـن المعـارض الجماعية الوطنية والدولية، ومـن أبرزها "باب جدة" في قاعة الفـن النقـي فـي حافـظ غاليـري بالريـاض، المملكة العربية السـعودية (2016)؛ معرض شارة الفني في حافظ غاليـري بجـدة، المملكة العربية السـعودية (2016)؛ "11 فنان سعودي" بالقاهرة، مصر (2002، 2010)؛ "الفـن للجميـع" فـي مؤسسـة المنصورية بجدة، المملكـة العربية السـعودية (2001)؛ بينالي الشـارقة الخامـس والسـادس، الإمـارات العربيـة المتحـدة (1999، 2001)؛ غاليـري قرية المفتاحة

بأبها، المملكة العربية السـعودية (1998)؛ معرض الفنانيـن العرب ببيروت، لبنان (1998)؛ معرض 25 فبراير بالكويت العاصمة، الكويت (1998)؛ النسختان الأولى والثانية من مسـابقة "وقـت الاختبار" بجدة، المملكة العربية السعودية (1994، 1995) ؛ الألوان لها إيقاع بجدة، المملكة العربية السـعودية (1995)؛ وميموري بوكس 2 بجدة، المملكة العربية السـعودية (1995). كمـا أقـام الزهرانـي العديد مـن المعارض الفرديـة، ومـن بينهـا معرض "شـقائق بغـداد" في حافظ غاليـري بجـدة، المملكة العربية السـعودية (2017)؛ ومعرض "ارتبـاط" فـي أتيليـيه جـدة، المملكـة العربيـة السـعودية (2004)؛ ومعـرض "مسـاحة تجريبية" بجـدة، المملكة العربية السـعودية (2000)؛ ومعـرض "3x3" فـي المركـز السـعودي للفنون التشـكيلية بجدة، المملكة العربية السـعودية (1998)، بالإضافـة إلى معرض مشـترك مع محمد الغامدي بعنوان "مسـافة" في حافظ غاليري بجدة، المملكة العربية السـعودية (2015). هذا وقد رعت مؤسسة المنصورية مشاركته بإقامة فنية في باريس نظّم خلالهـا معرضاً فرديـاً بعنوان "مصائر" (2004).

دخلـت أعمالـه إلـى المجموعـات الفنيـة فـي مؤسسـة المنصوريـة فـي جـدة بالمملكـة العربيـة السـعودية ووزارة الخارجيـة السـعودية.

OMAR ALZAHRANI

(b. 1969, Saudi Arabia)
Lives and works in Jeddah,
Saudi Arabia

Omar Alzahrani, previously known as Awdh Alzahraini, is a painter who grew up in Makkah. He was fascinated by the diversity of people visiting the city, which led him to translate their influences into his art. He earned a master's degree in art education from Umm Al-Qura University in Makkah. After graduating, he delved into the arts through his participation in seminars at multiple organizations, including Jeddah Atelier and the Tasami Center for Visual Art. The artist's Abstract Expressionist paintings convey heightened emotional states through his compositions. Influenced by the diverse sensory experiences of Makkah, his work draws inspiration from the city's vibrant voices, sounds, and scents. Evoking specific moments in time, he uses depth of color, expressive textures, and exaggerated brushstrokes to capture the mood and atmosphere of these histories. Alzahrani's dynamic brushstrokes create large movements across his canvases—not confined to a singular direction, but designed to elicit strong emotional responses from the viewer.

The artist has participated in several national and international group exhibitions, including *Bab Jeddah*, L'Art Pur, Hafez Gallery, Riyadh, Saudi Arabia (2016); Shara Art Fair, Hafez Gallery, Jeddah, Saudi Arabia (2016); *11 Saudi Artists*, Cairo, Egypt (2002, 2010); *Art for All*, Al-Mansouria Foundation, Jeddah, Saudi Arabia (2001); Sharjah Biennial 5 and 6, UAE (1999, 2001); Muftaha Village Gallery, Abha, Saudi Arabia (1998); *Arab Artists Exhibition*, Beirut, Lebanon (1998); *25th February Exhibition*, Kuwait City, Kuwait (1998); the first and second editions of *Quiz Time*, Jeddah, Saudi Arabia (1994, 1995); *Colours Have a Rhythm*, Jeddah, Saudi Arabia (1995); and *Memory Box II*, Jeddah, Saudi Arabia (1995). Alzahrani has also held several solo exhibitions, including *Sisters of Baghdad*, Hafez Gallery, Jeddah, Saudi Arabia (2017); *Correlation*, Atelier Jeddah, Saudi Arabia (2004); *Experimental Space*, Jeddah, Saudi Arabia (2000); and *3x3*, Saudi Center for Fine Art, Jeddah, Saudi Arabia (1998), as well as a joint exhibition with Mohammed AlGhamdi titled *Distance*, Hafez Gallery, Jeddah, Saudi Arabia (2015). In addition, the Al-Mansouria Foundation sponsored him to partake in a residency in Paris, during which he held a solo exhibition titled *Masayer* (2004).

His works are in the collections of the Al-Mansouria Foundation, Jeddah, Saudi Arabia and the Ministry of Foreign Affairs, Saudi Arabia.

OMAR ALZAHRANI
(b. 1969, Saudi Arabia)

Selfie, 2016

Canvas and plastic
140 × 200 cm
Courtesy of the artist

عمــر الزهرانــي
(مواليد 1969، المملكة العربية السعودية)

سلفي، 2016

قماش ولدائن
200 × 140 سم
بإذن من الفنان

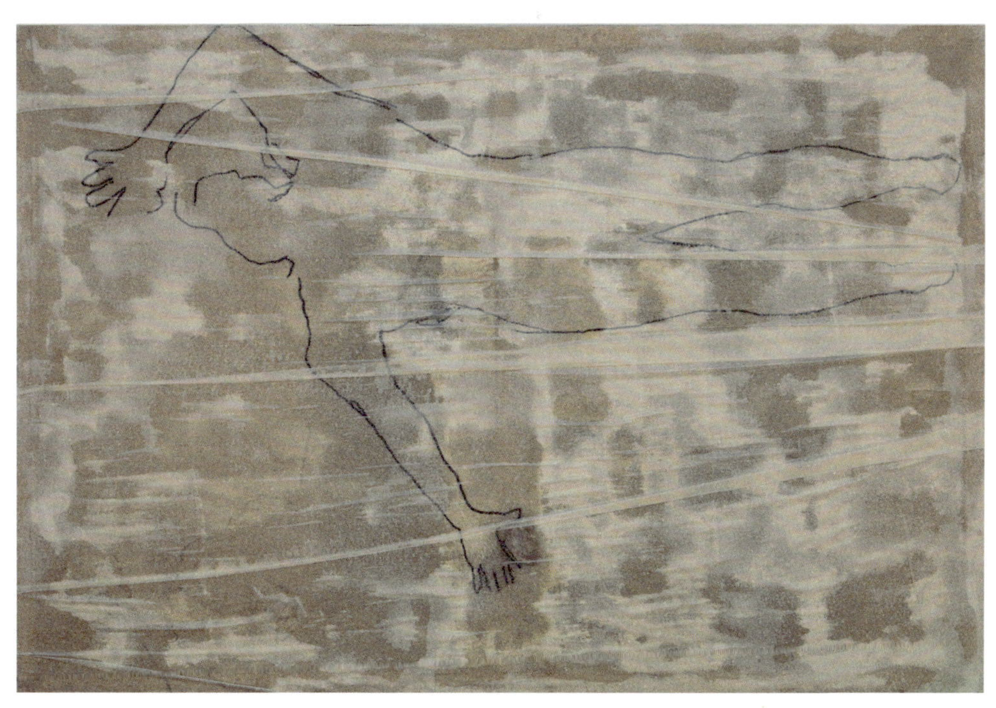

محمــــد شـــــرورو

(مواليد 1991، المغرب)
يقيم ويعمل في الدار البيضاء
(المغرب)

محمـد شـرورو هـو فنانٌ مفاهيمـي، انطلـق باستكشـافاته ودراسـاته من فضاء مواقـع الانترنت، وهو معروف بكونه من روّاد الحركة الفنية المسماة "الجمالية المغربية الجديدة" وقد تجلت مساهمته الرئيسية من خلال نشاطه في مجموعة رادار، حيث عمل من عام 2009 إلى عام 2014، وبالتالي أصبح أحد رواد حركة مـا بعد الإنترنت في المغرب. وعلى مـر السـنين، واصـل تعميـق أبحاثـه في استكشـاف الانتشـار الكلي للتدرجـات اللونية فـي العالم الرقمي، وتحديـاً منـه للـذكاء البشـري والـذكاء الاصطناعي، راح يرسـم أشـكالاً متدرجة الألـوان مكيّفـاً إياها إلى مـا لا نهاية.

شـارك في العديـد مـن المعـارض الجماعية، ومـن أبرزها "رسـم من المغرب، آآآه" فـي معرض باريـس الدولـي، فرنسـا (2023)؛ "معـاً مـن أجـل المغرب" في متحف محمد السادس للفن الحديث والمعاصر بالرباط، المغرب (2023)؛ "في المملكة" فـي مرسـى منطقـة التصميـم بميامـي، الولايات المتحـدة الأمريكيـة (2019)؛ "أولـى الرسـومات مـن الإنترنـت العربـي" في غاليـري فينيـس كادر بالـدار البيضـاء (GVCC)، المغرب (2016)؛ "نور القـرن"، بينالـي غوانجـو، كوريا الجنوبيـة (2015)؛ "ماسـترمايند 1" في غاليـري فينيـس كادر بالـدار البيضـاء (GVCC)، المغرب (2012). وتشـمل معارضـه الفرديـة "تدرجـات الإنترنـت" في غاليري فينيـس كادر بالـدار البيضـاء (GVCC)، المغرب (2021)؛ "كود ريفيو" في غاليري فينيس كادر بالدار البيضـاء (GVCC)، المغـرب (2022)؛ "تدرجـات الإنترنـت 1" في غاليـري فينيس كادر بالـدار البيضاء (GVCC)، المغرب (2018).

دخلـت أعماله إلى العديـد مـن المجموعات الفنيـة الهامـة مثل مركـز بومبيدو بباريس، فرنسـا؛ ومتحف محمد السـادس للفن الحديث والمعاصر بالرباط، المغرب؛ ومؤسسة برجيل للفنون بالشارقة، الإمارات العربية المتحدة؛ وR42 بسان فرانسيسكو، الولايـات المتحدة الأمريكية.

MOHAMMED CHROURO

(b. 1991, Morocco)
Lives and works in
Casablanca, Morocco

Mohammed Chrouro is a conceptual artist whose early explorations and studies come to life primarily within the virtual space of websites. He is recognized as the precursor of the artistic movement called "New Moroccan Aestheticism." His major contribution was illustrated within the Radar collective, where he worked from 2009 to 2014, thus becoming one of the pioneers of the post-Internet movement in Morocco. Over the years, the artist has continued to deepen his research into exploring the omnipresence of gradients in the digital world. As a challenge from human intelligence to artificial intelligence, he paints gradient shapes that he adapts to infinity.

Chrouro has participated in group exhibitions, including *A Drawing for Morocco*, Aaahhh!!! Paris Internationale, France (2023); *Unis pour le Maroc*, Mohammed VI Museum of Modern and Contemporary Art, Rabat, Morocco (2023); *In the Kingdom*, the Arsenale of Design District Space, Miami, USA (2019); *First Drawings from The Arab Internet*, GVCC Gallery, Casablanca, Morocco (2016); *Light of Century*, Gwangju Biennale, South Korea (2015); and *Mastermind 1*, GVCC Gallery, Casablanca, Morocco (2012) among others. Selected solo exhibitions include *The Gradients of Internet*, GVCC Gallery, Casablanca, Morocco (2021); *Code Review*, GVCC Gallery, Casablanca, Morocco (2022); and *The Dégradés of the Internet 1*, GVCC Gallery, Casablanca, Morocco (2018).

The artist's work is part of multiple public collections, namely Centre Pompidou, Paris, France; the Mohammed VI Museum of Modern and Contemporary Art, Rabat, Morocco; the Barjeel Art Foundation, Sharjah, UAE; and R42 San Francisco, USA.

محمـــد شـــرورو

(مواليد 1991، المغرب)

تدرجات الإنترنت *10*، 2015

ألوان زيتية على قماش
165 × 130 سم
بإذن مـن الفنان وغاليري فينيس كادر في الدار البيضاء

MOHAMMED CHROURO

(b. 1991, Morocco)

The Gradients of the Internet X, 2015

Oil on canvas
165 × 130 cm
Courtesy of the artist and GVCC Gallery, Casablanca

MOHAMMED CHROURO

(b. 1991, Morocco)

The Gradients of the Internet XIII, 2015

Oil on canvas
165 × 130 cm
Courtesy of the artist and GVCC Gallery, Casablanca

تدرجات الإنترنت 14، 2018

ألوان زيتية على قماش
165 × 130 سم
بإذن مــن الفنان وغاليري فينيس كادر في الدار البيضاء

MOHAMMED CHROURO

The Gradients of the Internet XIV, 2018

Oil on canvas
165 × 130 cm
Courtesy of the artist and GVCC Gallery, Casablanca

أيمــن يســري ديدبــان

(من مواليد 1966، فلسطين)
يقيم ويعمل في جدة
(المملكة العربية السعودية)

يركـز أيمـن يسـري ديدبـان في المقـام الأول علـى الهويـة والعلاقـات (بين الإنسـان والبيئة البشرية) والسـفر وعبور الحدود والصراعات الداخلية وقضايا النـوع الاجتماعـي والزمـن، وتتمحـور مزاولتـه الفنية متعـددة التخصصات حـول تفكيـك السـرديات الوطنيـة مـن منظـار "الحـارس" أو "الرقيـب". وقد اسـتخدم الفيديو في أعمالـه المبكرة بصفته شكلًا فنيـاً، وتعمـق في التصويـر الفوتوغرافـي والرسـم والنحـت والموسـيقى والأداء والتركيـب، وبـرع في دمـج الأسـاليب المفاهيميـة للتعبيـر عـن الأفكار العميقـة حـول الهيـاكل الاجتماعيـة والاقتصادية، متأرجحاً بين احترام الأنظمة القائمة والتشكيك بها.

شـارك ديدبـان في العديـد مـن المعارض الجماعيـة، مـن أبرزها بينالـي الفنون الإسلامية في جـدة، المملكـة العربية السـعودية (2023)؛ وبينالي الدرعيـة في الريـاض، المملكـة العربيـة السـعودية (2021)؛ و"نـور علـى نـور"، في احتفال نـور الرياض، المملكة العربيـة السـعودية (2021)؛ و"صورة زمنية: لمحة عامـة لفـن الفيديـو فـي المملكـة العربيـة السـعودية" فـي غاليري أثر بجـدة، المملكة العربية السـعودية (2020)؛ وبينالي القاهرة، مصر (2019)؛ و"المركـز العاشـر: الفـن السـعودي المعاصـر" في المتحف العربي الأمريكي الوطني بديترويت، الولايات المتحـدة الأمريكيـة (2017)؛ و"فانتـم بنـش: فـن معاصـر من المملكة العربية السـعودية" في متحف كليـة بايتس للفنون بلوويسـتون، الولايـات المتحدة الأمريكيـة (2016)؛ و"الحـج إلـى مكة" فـي معهد العالـم العربي بباريـس، فرنسا (2014)؛ و"الحنين إلى مكة" في المتحف الوطني للإثنولوجيا بلايدن، هولنـدا (2013)؛ و"الحـج: رحلة إلى قلب الإسـلام" فـي المتحـف البريطانـي بلنـدن، المملكة المتحدة

(2012)؛ وبينالـي البندقية، إيطاليا (2011)؛ و"حافة الجزيرة العربية" في قاعة بروناي في كلية الدراسات الشـرقية والإفريقيـة فـي جامعـة لنـدن، المملكـة المتحـدة (2008)، أمـا معارضه الفردية فتتضمّن "أعطنـي الضـوء" فـي غاليـري أثر بجـدة، المملكة العربيـة السـعودية (2016)؛ و"أرض مشـتركة" في غاليري صابرينا عمراني بمدريد، إسـبانيا (2014)؛ و"أنا أي شـيء وأنا كل شـيء" في غاليري أثر بجدة، المملكة العربيـة السـعودية (2012)؛ و"الهوية" فـي غاليري سـلمى فريانـي بلنـدن، المملكة المتحـدة (2011).

دخلـت أعمالـه إلـى العديـد مـن المجموعـات الفنيـة، ومنهـا مجموعـة مؤسسـة المنصوريـة في جـدة بالمملكة العربية السـعودية؛ ومتحف بسـمة السـليمان للفن المعاصر (بسـموكا) بجدة، المملكة العربيـة السـعودية؛ ومركـز بومبيدو بباريس، فرنسا؛ والمتحـف البريطانـي بلنـدن، المملكـة المتحـدة؛ ومتحـف "الصنـدوق الأخضر" للفـن السـعودي المعاصـر بأمسـتردام، هولندا.

AYMAN YOSSRI DAYDBAN

(b. 1966, Palestine)
Lives and works in Jeddah,
Saudi Arabia

Ayman Yossri Daydban focuses primarily on identity, relationships (between man and the human environment), travel, crossing borders, internal conflicts, gender issues, and time. His multidisciplinary practice revolves around the deconstruction of national narratives with the approach of a watchman or guard. Early on, the artist used video as an art form, and he has also delved into photography, painting, sculpture, music, performance, and installation. Ingeniously incorporating conceptual ways to express visceral ideas about our socioeconomic structures, he wavers between respect for existing systems and a deep questioning of them.

Daydban's group shows have included the Islamic Arts Biennale, Jeddah, Saudi Arabia (2023); Diriyah Biennale, Riyadh, Saudi Arabia (2021); *Light Upon Light*, Noor Riyadh, Saudi Arabia (2021); *Durational Portrait: A Brief Overview of Video Art in Saudi Arabia*, Athr Gallery, Jeddah, Saudi Arabia (2020); Cairo Biennale, Egypt (2019); *Epicenter X: Contemporary Saudi Art*, Arab American National Museum, Detroit, USA (2017); *Phantom Punch: Contemporary Art from Saudi Arabia*, Bates College Museum of Art, Lewiston, USA (2016); *Hajj: The Pilgrimage to Mecca*, Institut du monde arabe, Paris, France (2014); *Longing for Mecca: A Pilgrim's Journey*, Rijksmuseum Volkenkunde, Leiden, The Netherlands (2013); *Hajj: Journey to the Heart of Islam*, British Museum, London, UK (2012); 54th Venice Biennale, Italy (2011); and *Edge of Arabia*, Brunei Gallery, SOAS University of London, UK (2008), among others.

His solo exhibitions have included *Give Me the Light*, Athr Gallery, Jeddah, Saudi Arabia (2016); *Common Grounds*, Sabrina Amrani Gallery, Madrid, Spain (2014); *I Am Anything, I Am Everything*, Athr Gallery, Jeddah, Saudi Arabia (2012); and *Identity*, Selma Feriani, London, UK (2011).

His work is part of the collections of the Al-Mansouria Foundation, Jeddah, Saudi Arabia; the Basma Al Sulaiman Museum of Contemporary Art (BASMOCA), Jeddah, Saudi Arabia; the Centre Pompidou, Paris, France; the British Museum, London, UK; and the Greenbox Museum of Contemporary Art from Saudi Arabia, Amsterdam, The Netherlands.

AYMAN YOSSRI DAYDBAN
(b. 1966, Palestine)

Somewhere Beautiful, 2021

Video installation
Dimensions variable
Courtesy of the artist

أيـــن يسـري ديدبـان
(مواليد 1966، فلسطين)

مكان ما جميل، 2021

تركيب فني باستخدام الفيديو
مقاسات مختلفة
بإذن من الفنان

تعتمد على سمعها القوي للإحساس بالخطر

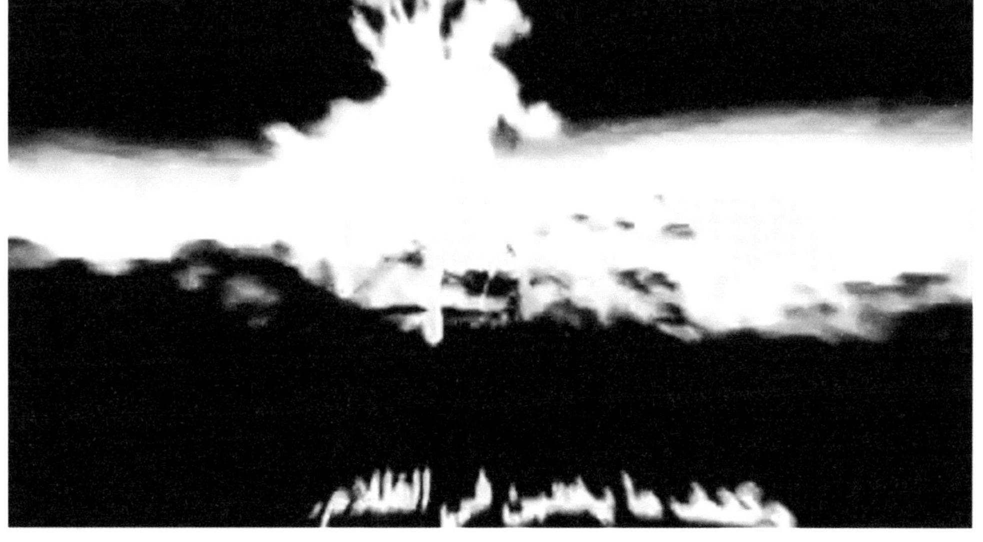
تعرف ما يحدث في الظلام

إيمـان الجبريـن

(مواليد 1981،
المملكة العربية السعودية)
تقيم وتعمل في الرياض
(المملكة العربية السعودية)

إيمـان الجبريـن هي فنانـةٌ وقيّمـة فنيـة متعددة التخصصات تـرأس حاليـاً لجنـة الثقافة والرياضة والسـياحة فـي مجلـس الشـورى السـعودي فـي الريـاض، واشـتهرت بإسـهاماتها الكبيرة في المشهد الفني السـعودي كفنانة ومعلمة، وهي حاصلة على درجة الدكتـوراه في تاريخ الفـن الحديث والمعاصر مـن جامعـة ساسـكس فـي المملكـة المتحـدة فـي عـام 2014، ودرجـة الماجسـتير فـي تعليـم الفـن مـن جامعـة الملـك سـعود فـي المملكة العربيـة السـعودية فـي عـام 2006، وقـد أوصلتهـا هـذه الثـروة المعرفيـة إلـى العمـل ككاتبـة فـي جريـدة الريـاض وجريـدة الجزيـرة اليوميـة، حيـث نشـرت المقالات وحـررت أخبـار المعـارض، وعملت منذ عام 2015 كأسـتاذة مسـاعدة لتاريـخ الفن فـي جامعة الأميرة نورة بنـت عبدالرحمن بالرياض، كما تعاونت كباحثـة ومستشـارة فنيـة فـي العديد من مشـاريع الفـن السـعودي مـع متحـف الفـن الحديـث فـي نيويـورك، وآرت دبي مودرن، ومركز الملك عبدالعزيز الثقافي العالمـي (إثراء)، ودارة صفية بن زقر بجدة، ودار الفنون السـعودية. فضلاً عـن ذلك، اضطلعت الجبريـن بالإشـراف على تنظيم عدد مـن الفعاليات الفنيـة البـارزة، كاحتفال نور الرياض (2021) والجناح الوطنـي السـعودي فـي بينالـي البندقيـة الثامـن والخمسين (2019)، وتهدف من أعمالها إلى تفنيد الصور النمطيـة والمفاهيـم الخاطئـة الغربيـة عن المـرأة السـعودية والثقافة السـعودية بشـكل عام.

شـاركت فـي العديد مـن المعارض الجماعية محليـاً ودوليـاً، ومـن أبرزهـا "العالـم عبارة عـن منديـل" فـي غاليـري اسـتوديو لنـدن للطباعـة، المملكـة المتحـدة، وهو معـرض تنقّل بيـن عمّان،

الأردن (مؤسسـة محمـد وماهـرة أبـو غزالة للفن والثقافة) ونيويـورك، الولايات المتحـدة الأمريكية (مؤسسة إليزابيـث) وقرطبة، الأرجنتيـن (متحف بونفيليولي) (2022-2020)؛ و"وسـم" في معهد مسـك للفنون بالرياض، المملكة العربية السعودية (2020)؛ و"دبي تلتقي بالعالم" في غاليري عائشة العبار بدبي، الإمارات العربية المتحـدة (2018)؛ فـن جـدة 21,39 فـي المجلـس الفني السـعودي، المملكة العربية السعودية (2016)؛ بينالي البندقية الخامس والخمسـون، إيطاليا (2013)؛ و"السـفير" فـي باريـس، فرنسـا (2010)؛ و"جمع المؤنث" فـي السـفارة الفرنسـية بالريـاض، المملكـة العربية السـعودية (2008).

حصلت الجبريـن على العديـد مـن الجوائز، منها جائزة آرت باريس (2018)؛ والميدالية الفضية لورينـزو العظيـم فـي بينالـي فلورنسا (2015)؛ وجائـزة بيـان الهويـة مـن جامعـة برونيـل، لندن، المملكة المتحدة (2012)؛ والمعرض الوطني الرابع للفنانـات السـعوديات، الرياض، المملكة العربية السـعودية (2008)؛ ومعـرض الوعـلان الوطنـي الثالث، الرياض، المملكة العربية السعودية، 2002.

EIMAN ELGIBREEN

(b. 1981, Saudi Arabia)
Lives and works in Riyadh,
Saudi Arabia

Eiman Elgibreen is a multidisciplinary artist and curator as well as the former chair of the Culture, Sports, and Tourism Committee of the Saudi Shura Council in Riyadh, Saudi Arabia. Recognized for her significant contributions to the Saudi art scene as both an artist and a teacher, she obtained her DPhil in modern and contemporary art history from the University of Sussex in the UK in 2014 and a master's in art education from King Saud University in Saudi Arabia in 2006. This wealth of knowledge brought her to hold roles as a writer for *Al-Riyadh* and the *Al-Jazirah Daily Newspaper*, publishing articles and exhibition reviews. Since 2015, she has worked as an assistant professor of art history at the Princess Nourah bint Abdulrahman University in Riyadh. She has also collaborated as a researcher and an art consultant on various Saudi art projects with the Museum of Modern Art in New York, USA; Art Dubai Modern, UAE; Barjeel Foundation, UAE; Misk Art Institute, KSA; the Ithra World Center, KSA; the Diriyah Gate Authority, KSA; the Royal Commission of Riyadh City, KSA; Darat Safeya Binzagr, Jeddah, Saudi Arabia; and Dar Al-funoon Al-Saudia, and she curated notable exhibitions, including the Noor Riyadh festival (2021) and the National Pavilion of Saudi Arabia at the 58th Venice Biennale (2019). Her work aims to contest Western stereotypes and misconceptions about Saudi women and Saudi culture in general.

Elgibreen has participated in numerous group exhibitions locally and internationally. Notable presentations include *The World Is a Handkerchief* at London Print Studio Gallery, UK, a traveling exhibition that was also shown in Amman, Jordan (MMAG Foundation); New York, USA (Elizabeth Foundation); and Cordoba, Argentina (Bonfiglioli Museum) (2020–2022), in addition to *Imprint*, Misk Art Institute, Riyadh, Saudi Arabia (2020); *Dubai Meets the World*, Aisha Alabbar Gallery, Dubai, UAE (2018); 21, 39 Jeddah Arts, Saudi Art Council, Saudi Arabia (2016); 55th Venice Biennale, Italy (2013); *Assafeer*, Paris, France (2010); and *Feminine Plural*, French Embassy, Riyadh, Saudi Arabia (2008).

The artist has received several awards, including Art Paris (2018); the Lorenzo il Magnifico silver medal, Florence Biennale (2015); the Statement of Identity award at Brunel University, London, UK (2012); the 4th National Exhibition for Saudi Women Artists, Riyadh, Saudi Arabia (2008); and the Wa'alan 3rd National Exhibition, Riyadh, Saudi Arabia, 2002.

إيمــــان الجبريــــن
(مواليد 1981، المملكة العربية السعودية)

عذراً سيدتي، هل ضللت الطريق؟
(سلسلة الأقنعة الإلكترونية)، 2017

طبعة رقمية، خشب، وبليكسي جلاس
50 × 60 سم
بإذن من الفنانة

EIMAN ELGIBREEN
(b. 1981, Saudi Arabia)

Excuse Me Miss, Are You Lost?
(Electronic Veils Series), 2017

Digital print, wood, and Plexiglas
50 × 60 cm
Courtesy of the artist

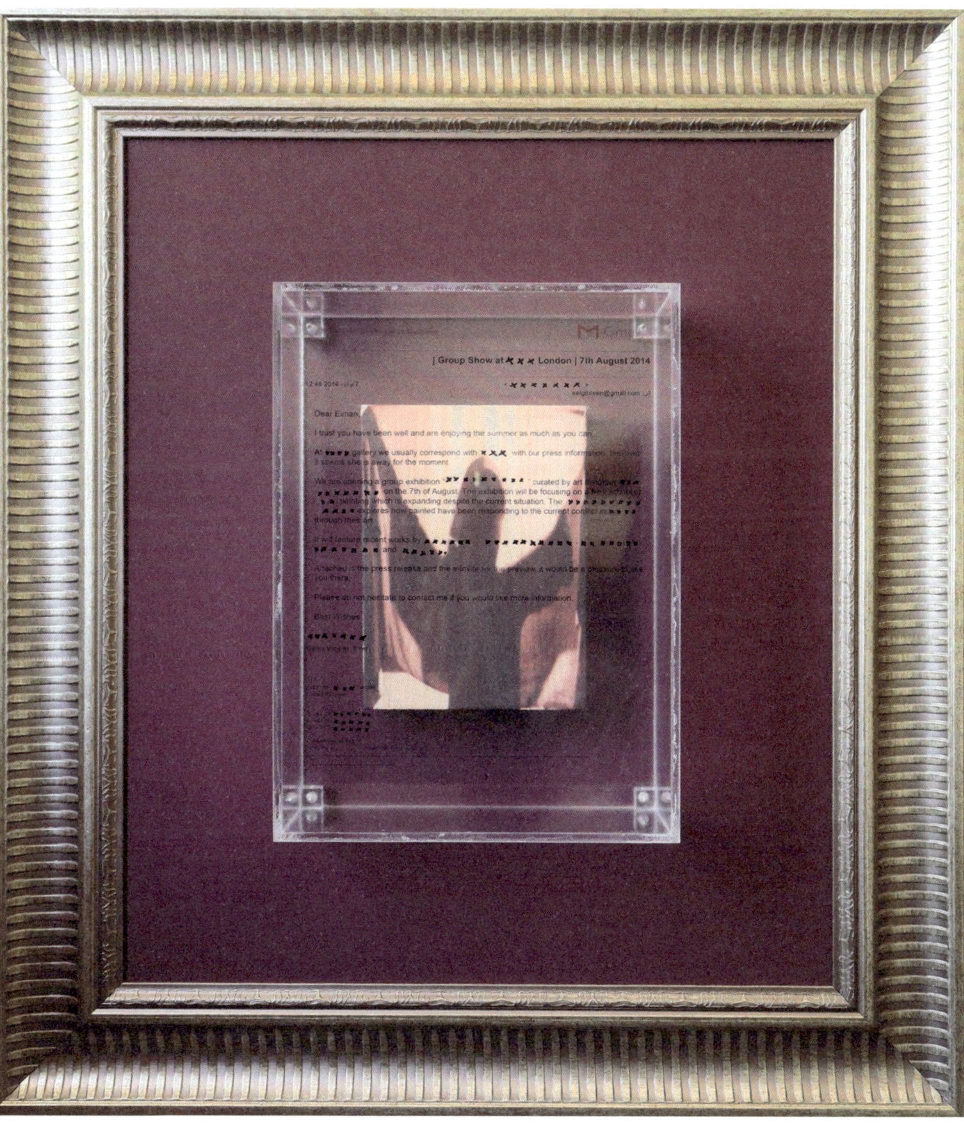

| Group Show at ✗ ✗ ✗ London | 7th August 2014
eelgibreen@gmail.com

Dear Eiman,

I trust you have been well and are enjoying the summer as much as you can.

At ✗✗✗ gallery we usually correspond with ✗ ✗✗ with our press information. However it seems she is away for the moment.

We are opening a group exhibition "✗✗ ✗ ✗ ✗ ✗ ✗ ✗" curated by art historian ✗ ✗ ✗ ✗ ✗ ✗ ✗ ✗ ✗ on the 7th of August. The exhibition will be focusing on a field of study of ✗ ✗ painting which is expanding despite the current situation. The ✗ ✗ ✗ ✗ ✗ ✗ ✗ ✗ explores how painted have been responding to the current conflict in ✗ ✗ ✗ through their art.

It will feature recent works by ✗ and ✗ ✗ ✗ ✗.

Attached is the press release and the e-invite for the preview, it would be a pleasure to see you there.

Please do not hesitate to contact me if you would like more information.

Best Wishes,

✗ ✗ ✗ ✗ ✗ ✗

EIMAN ELGIBREEN

(b. 1981, Saudi Arabia)

So She Is Open-Minded and You Are...? (Electronic Veils Series), 2017

Digital print, wood, and Plexiglas
50 × 60 cm
Courtesy of the artist

إيمـــــان الجبريــــن

(مواليد 1981، المملكة العربية السعودية)

إذن هي ذات العقل المنفتح وأنت...؟
(سلسلة الأقنعة الإلكترونية)، 2017

طبعة رقمية، خشب، وبليكسي جلاس
50 × 60 سم
بإذن من الفنانة

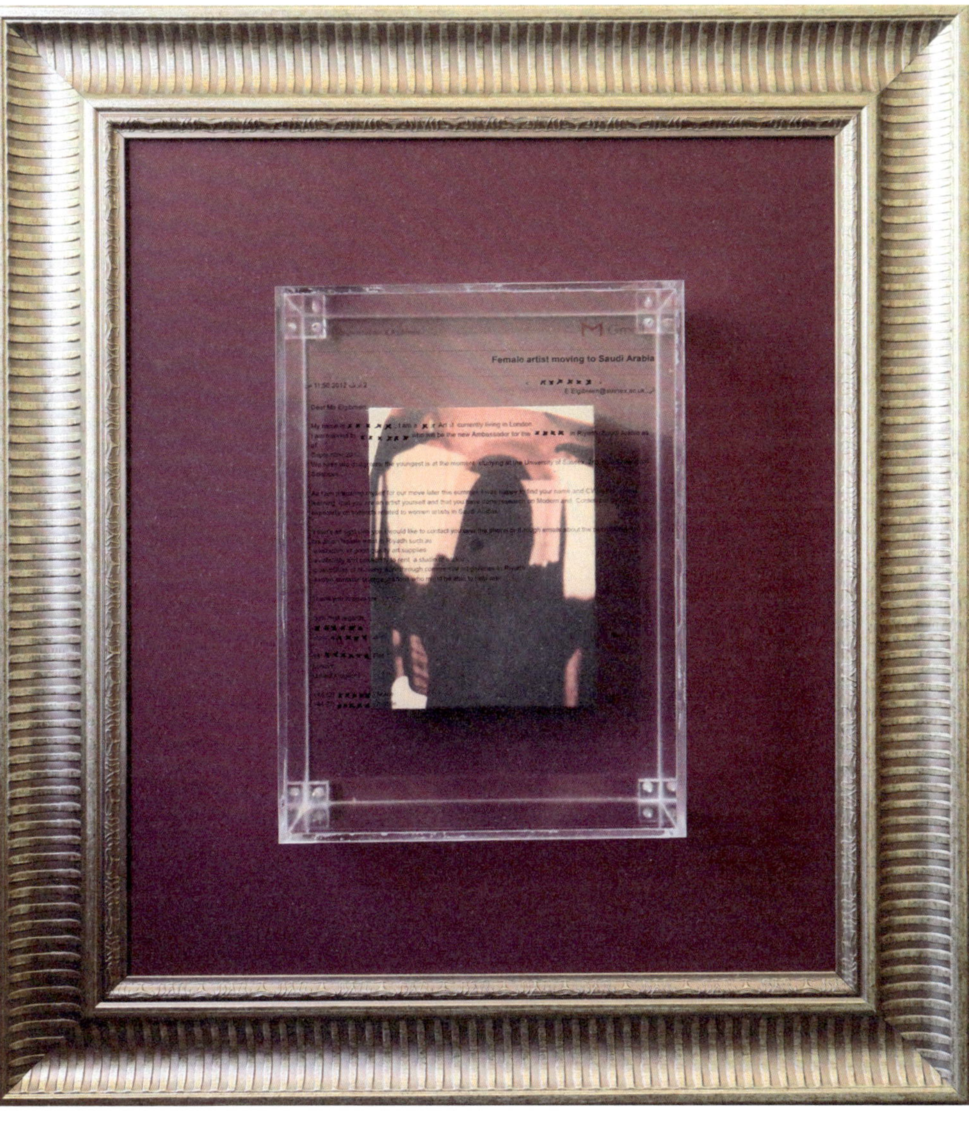

Female artist moving to Saudi Arabia

11:58 2012 ✕✕✕✕✕
E.Elgibreen@sussex.ac.uk

Dear Ms Elgibreen

My name is ✕✕✕✕✕, I am a ✕✕✕ Art ✕ currently living in London.
I am married to ✕✕✕✕✕ who will be the new Ambassador for the ✕✕✕✕ in Riyadh, Saudi Arabia as of September 20✕✕.
We have ✕✕ children, the youngest is at the moment studying at the University of Sussex, 2nd ✕✕✕ BA ✕✕ Sciences.

As I am preparing myself for our move later this summer, I was happy to find your name and CV ✕✕✕ and I learned that you are an artist yourself and that you have done research on Modern and Contemporary ✕✕✕✕ especially on ✕✕✕✕✕ related to women artists in Saudi Arabia.

I would very much wish you would like to contact you over the phone or through email about the best ✕✕✕✕✕✕ in the art ✕✕✕✕ market in Riyadh such as
- availability of good quality art supplies
- availability and possibility to rent a studio for work
- possibilities of showing work through commercial art galleries in Riyadh
- another contact or someone who might be able to help me

I look ✕✕✕ regards,

✕✕✕✕✕✕
✕✕✕✕✕✕✕

Tel ✕✕✕✕✕✕ Fax
London
United Kingdom

+44 (0) ✕✕✕✕✕ (home)
+44 (0) ✕✕✕✕✕ (mobile)

إيمـــان الجبريـــن

(مواليد 1981، المملكة العربية السعودية)

كنت اعتقد أنكَ رجل أيرلندي ضخم! (سلسلة الأقنعة الإلكترونية)، 2017

طبعة رقمية، خشب، وبليكسي جلاس

50 × 60 سم

بإذن من الفنانة

EIMAN ELGIBREEN

(b. 1981, Saudi Arabia)

I Thought You Were a Big Irish Guy! (Electronic Veil Series), 2017

Digital print, wood, and Plexiglas
50 × 60 cm
Courtesy of the artist

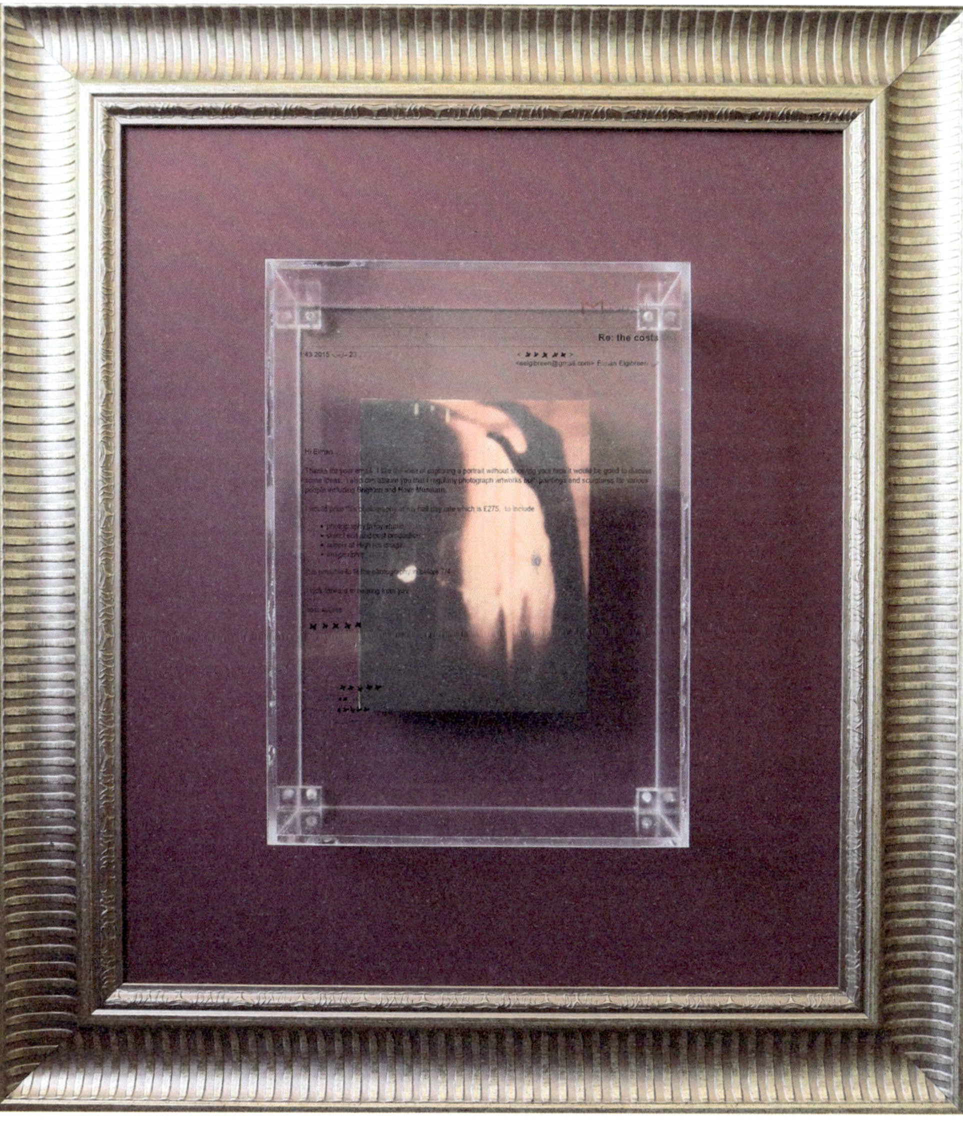

Re: the costs
143 2015 ... 23
<seeigibreen@gmail.com> Eiman Elgibreen
Hi Eiman
Thanks for your email. I like the idea of capturing a portrait without showing your face it would be good to discuss some ideas. I also can assure you that I regularly photograph artworks but paintings and sculptures for various people including Brighton and Hove Museums.
I would price the photography at my half day rate which is £275, to include
photography in my studio
shoot edit and post production
sample of high res image
image rights
I'm sure I can fit the photography in before 7/4
I look forward to hearing from you
Best wishes

إيمـــان الجبريـــن

(مواليد 1981، المملكة العربية السعودية)

ظننت أنني مثلكَ تماماً...

(سلسلة الأقنعة الإلكترونية)، 2017

طبعة رقمية، خشب، وبليكسي جلاس

50 × 60 سم

بإذن من الفنانة

EIMAN ELGIBREEN

(b. 1981, Saudi Arabia)

I Am Just Like You, I Thought...
(Electronic Veil Series), 2017

Digital print, wood, and Plexiglas
50 × 60 cm
Courtesy of the artist

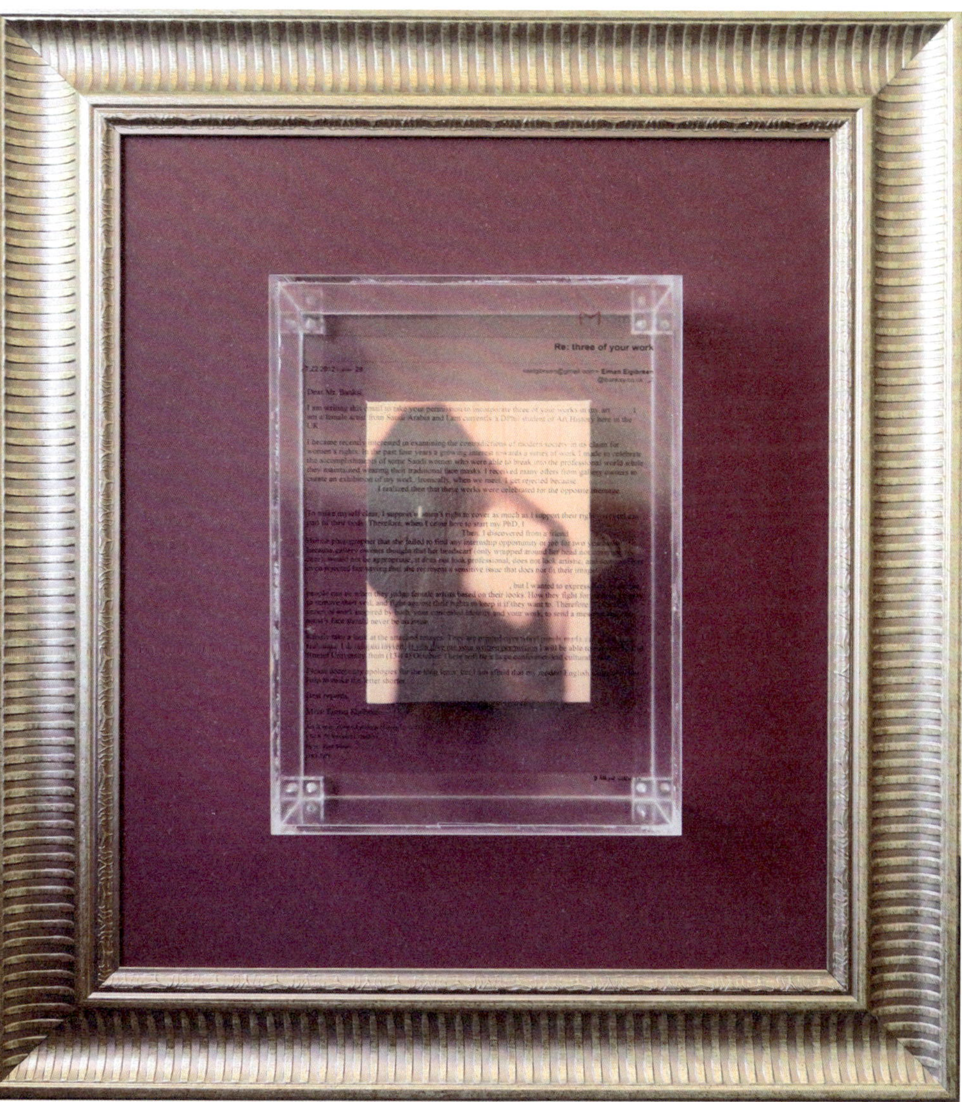

Re: three of your work

Dear Mr. Banksi,

I am writing this email to take your permission to incorporate three of your works in my art. I am a female artist from Saudi Arabia and I am currently a DPhil student of Art History here in the UK.

I became recently interested in examining the contradictions of modern society in its claim for women's rights. In the past four years a growing interest towards a series of work I made to celebrate the accomplishments of some Saudi women who were able to break into the professional world while they maintained wearing their traditional face masks. I received many offers from gallery owners to curate an exhibition of my work. Ironically, when we meet, I get rejected because

I realized then that these works were celebrated for the opposite message.

To make myself clear, I support women's right to cover as much as I support their right to reveal and to their body. Therefore, when I came here to start my PhD, I

Then, I discovered from a friend

female photographer that she failed to find any internship opportunity or job for two years because gallery owners thought that her headscarf (only wrapped around her head not covering her face), would not be appropriate, it does not look professional, does not look artistic, and some of them are co-rejected her viewing that she represents a sensitive issue that does not fit their image

, but I wanted to express

people can be when they judge female artists based on their looks. How they fight for woman's rights to remove their veil, and fight against their rights to keep it if they want to. Therefore art work inspired by both your concealed identity and your work, to send a message artist's face should never be an issue.

Kindly take a look at the attached images. They are printed copies that I made myself. If you give me your written permission I will be able to exhibit them from (13 to 4) October. There will be a large conference and cultural

Please accept my apologies for the long letter, but I am afraid that my modest English didn't help to make the letter shorter.

Best regards,

Miss Eman Elgibreen

منير فاطمي

(مواليد 1970، المغرب)
يقيم ويعمل بين باريس (فرنسا)
وطنجة (المغرب)

منير فاطمي فنانٌ معاصر معروف باستكشافه للإعلام والمجتمع. في سن السابعة عشرة، درس في المدرسة الحرة لرسم الجسد التابعة لأكاديمية الفنون الجميلة في روما. وفي عام 1989، التحق بمدرسة الفنون الجميلة في الدار البيضاء لفترة قصيرة، وبدأ مسيرته الفنية كمصمم جرافيكي في إحدى وكالات الإعلانات. وبعد ستة أعوام، رُقّع إلى منصب المدير الفني فيها، إلّا أنه سرعان ما ترك هذه الوظيفة ليتفرّغ للفن بالكامل، ففي عام 2006، حصل على منحة حكومية للدراسة في أكاديمية ريجكس بأمستردام، يستكشف فاطمي في مزاولته الفنية تقاطع التاريخ والتكنولوجيا والثقافة الشعبية والقضايا المجتمعية؛ ولذلك يستخدم في أعماله التركيبية مختلف المواد كالكابلات والآلات الكاتبة وأشرطة الفيديو، متعمّقاً في موضوعات الذاكرة واللغة والتواصل.

عُرضت أعماله في العديد من المعارض الجماعية، ومن أبرزها؛ "عالمنا يحترق" في قصر طوكيو بباريس، فرنسا (2020)؛ و"سوبر كلوب" في غاليري وايلد بازل، سويسرا (2020)؛ و"روايات صامتة" في متحف الفن المعاصر في ينتشوان، الصين (2019)؛ و"جناح المنفى – على هامش بينالي داكار" في المعهد الفرنسي في السنغال بسانت لويس، السنغال (2018)؛ و"عين على العالم العربي" في معهد العالم العربي بباريس، فرنسا (2018)؛ وبينالي البندقية السابع والخمسون، إيطاليا (2017)؛ و"منظر جوهري" في متحف المعدن للفن الأفريقي المعاصر بمراكش، المغرب (2016)؛ و"198920072016" في غاليري بابيلّون بباريس، فرنسا (2016)؛ و"اللمسة الحضرية" في قاعة فاوست للفنون بهانوفر، ألمانيا (2016)؛

لقاء باماكو العاشر، البينالي الأفريقي للتصوير الفوتوغرافي، مالي (2015)؛ وبينالي سالونيك الخامس، اليونان (2015)؛ و"مَن قال إن الغد ليس موجوداً؟"، البينالي الثلاثي الأول، ريو دي جانيرو، البرازيل (2015)؛ و"خلف الجدار 2"، بينالي هافانا - مشروع جانبي، الماليكون، كوبا (2015)؛ و"التسامح"، بينالي بودروم الدولي الثاني، تركيا (2015)؛ "H2M – صدى" بينالي ليون، بورغ أون بريس، فرنسا (2013)؛ بينالي البندقية الرابع والخمسون، إيطاليا (2011). وأقام أكثر من خمسين معرضاً فردياً من بينها "قصص هامسة لأسلاك منسية" في غاليري بييرو أتشوغاري بميامي، الولايات المتحدة الأمريكية (2023)؛ و"عصر العواقب" في مكتبة الصور بميلانو، إيطاليا (2021)؛ و"العامل البشري" في متحف طوكيو متروبوليتان تيين للفنون، اليابان (2018)؛ و"داخل دائرة النار" في غاليري لاوري شبيبي بدبي، الإمارات العربية المتحدة (2017).

دخلت أعماله إلى المجموعات الفنية لعدد من المؤسسات، مثل قاعة غرب أستراليا للفنون في بيرث بأستراليا؛ ومؤسسة لويس فيتون في باريس بفرنسا؛ ومتحف قصر الفنون في دوسلدورف بألمانيا؛ ومتحف بروكلين في نيويورك بالولايات المتحدة الأمريكية، ونالت أعماله تقديراً تمثّل في زمالة من الصندوق الوطني للفنون ومنحة من مؤسسة بولوك-كراسنر.

MOUNIR FATMI

(b. 1970, Morocco)
Lives and works in Paris,
France, and Tangier, Morocco

Mounir Fatmi is a contemporary artist known for his exploration of media and society. At the age of seventeen, he studied at the Scuola Libera delle Nudo (Free School of the Nude), part of the Accademia di Belle Arti in Rome, and in 1989, he enrolled in the School of Fine Arts of Casablanca for a short period. He began his career as a graphic designer at an advertising agency, and six years later, he advanced to the position of artistic director. Shortly thereafter, he left the role to become a full-time artist. In 2006, he received a government scholarship to study at the Rijksakademie in Amsterdam. Fatmi's practice explores the intersection of history and technology, popular culture, and societal issues. His installations therefore employ materials such as cables, type-writers, and VHS tapes, as they delve into themes of memory, language, and communication.

Fatmi's work has been featured in numerous group exhibitions, including *Our World Is Burning*, Palais de Tokyo, Paris, France (2020); *Supper Club*, Wilde Gallery, Basel, Switzerland (2020); *Silent Narratives*, Museum of Contemporary Art, Yinchuan, China (2019); *Le Pavillon de l'Exil—Off de la Biennale de Dakar*, Institut français du Sénégal à Saint Louis, Senegal (2018); *Un œil ouvert sur le monde arabe*, Institut du monde arabe, Paris, France (2018); the 57th Venice Biennale, Italy (2017); *Essentiel Paysage*, Musée d'art contemporain africain Al Maaden, Marrakech, Morocco (2016); *198920072016*, Galerie Papillon, Paris, France (2016); *Urban Touch*, Kunsthalle Faust, Hannover, Germany (2016); 10th Bamako Encounters, African Biennale of Photography, Mali (2015); 5th Thessaloniki Biennale, Greece (2015); *Who Said That Tomorrow Doesn't Exist?*, 1st Trio Biennial, Rio de Janeiro, Brazil (2015); *Detrás del Muro II*, Havana Biennial—Collateral Project, el Malecón, Cuba (2015); *Tolerance*, the 2nd International Bodrum Biennial, Turkey (2015); H2M—Résonance de la Biennale de Lyon, Bourg-en-Bresse, France (2013); and the 54th Venice Biennial, Italy (2011), among others. He has held more than fifty solo exhibitions; select presentations include *Whispered Stories of Forgotten Wires*, Piero Atchugarry Gallery, Miami, USA (2023); *The Age of Consequences*, Officine dell'Immagine, Milan, Italy (2021); *The Human Factor*, Tokyo Metropolitan Teien Art Museum, Japan (2018); and *Inside the Fire Circle*, Lawrie Shabibi, Dubai, UAE (2017).

The artist's work has been collected by institutions such as the Art Gallery of Western Australia, Perth, Australia; the Fondation Louis Vuitton, Paris, France; the Museum Kunstpalast, Düsseldorf, Germany; and the Brooklyn Museum, New York, USA. He has received recognition for his work, including National Endowment for the Arts Fellowships and a Pollock-Krasner Foundation Grant.

(مواليد 1970، المغرب)

المادة البيضاء، 2020-2021

ألوان وستيريو
16 دقيقة
بإذن من الفنان وغاليري لاوري شبيبي في دبي

MOUNIR FATMI
(b. 1970, Morocco)

The White Matter, 2020–2021

Color and stereo
16 min.
Courtesy of the artist and Lawrie Shabibi Gallery, Dubai

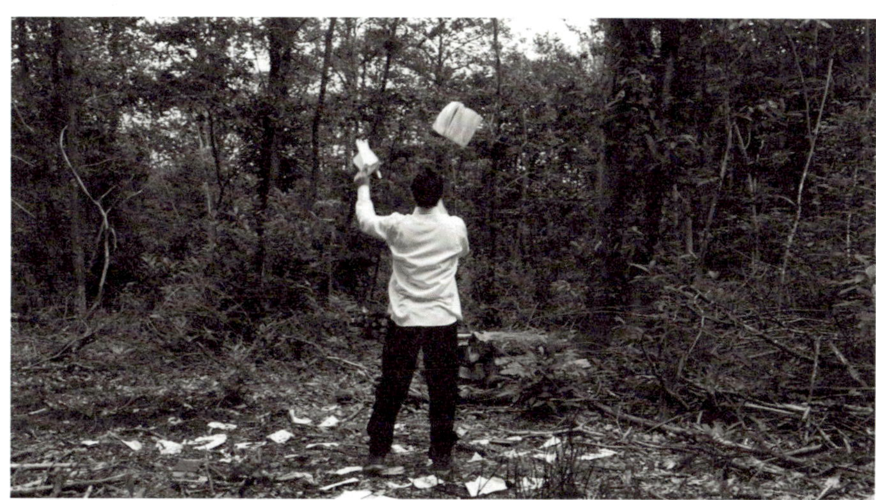

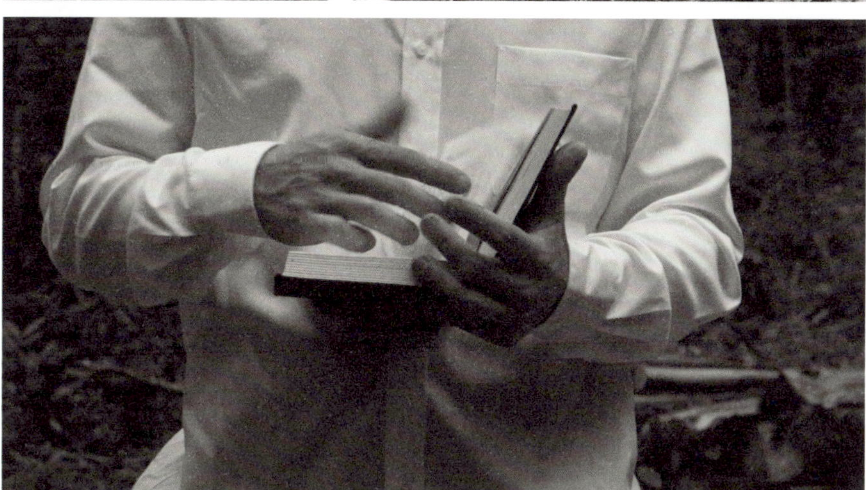

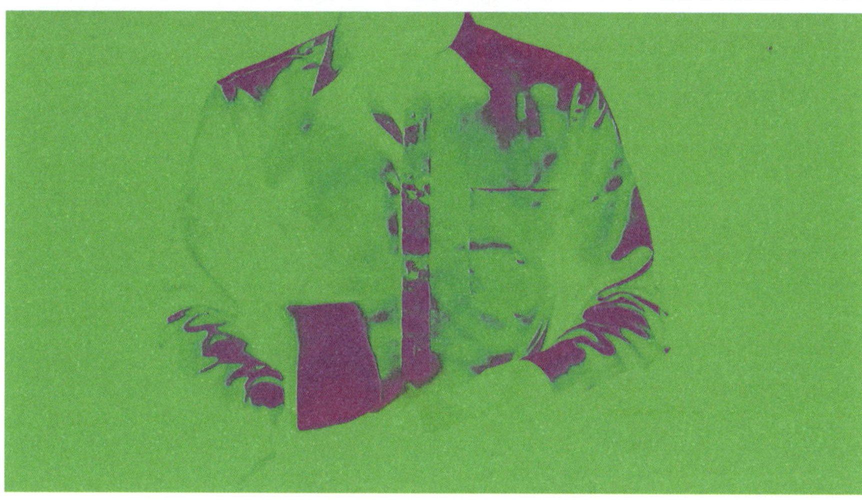

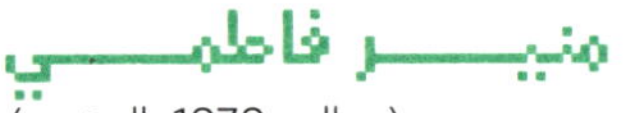

(مواليد 1970، المغرب)

داخل دائرة النار، 2017

آلات كاتبة، كابلات تشغيل، أوراق، طاولة
140 × 300 × 60 سم
بإذن من الفنان وغاليري لاوري شبيبي في دبي

MOUNIR FATMI

(b. 1970, Morocco)

Inside the Fire Circle, 2017

Typewriters, starter cables, papers, and table
140 × 300 × 60 cm
Courtesy of the artist and Lawrie Shabibi Gallery, Dubai

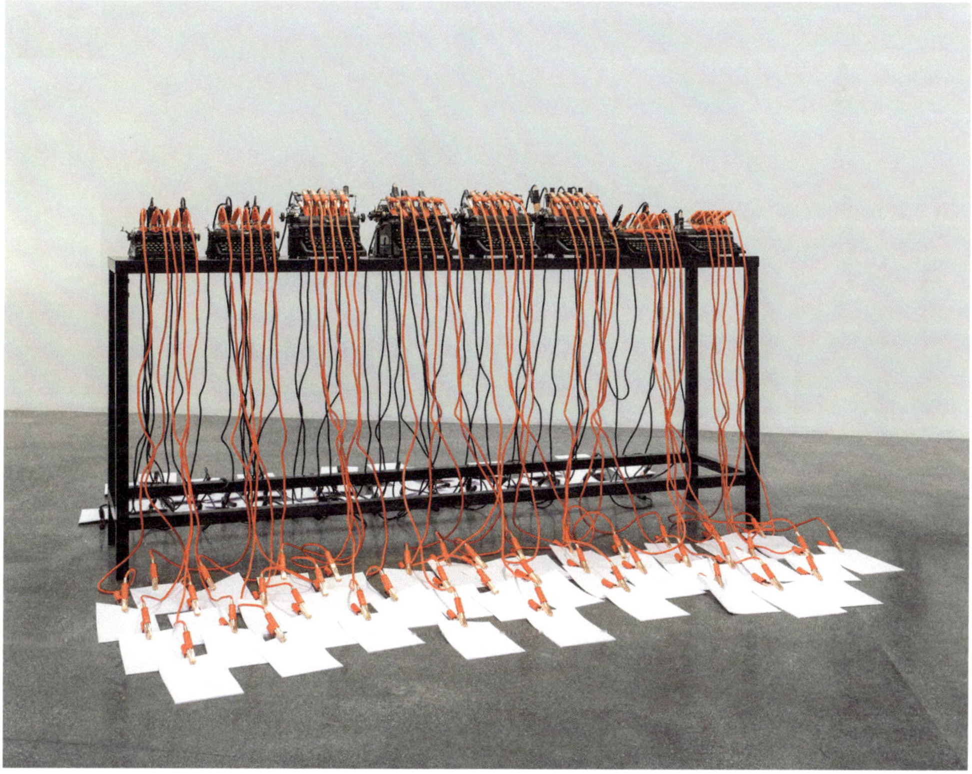

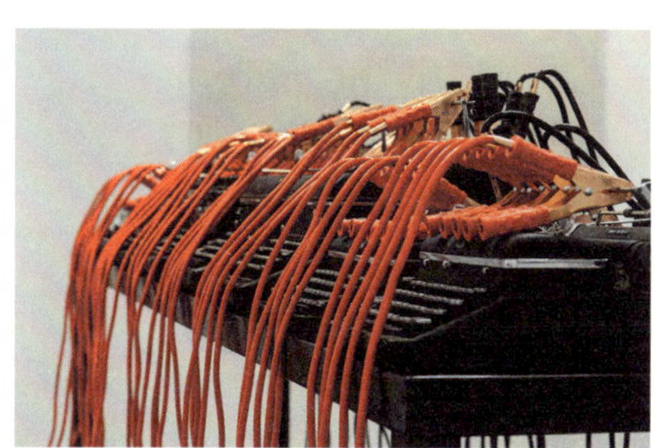
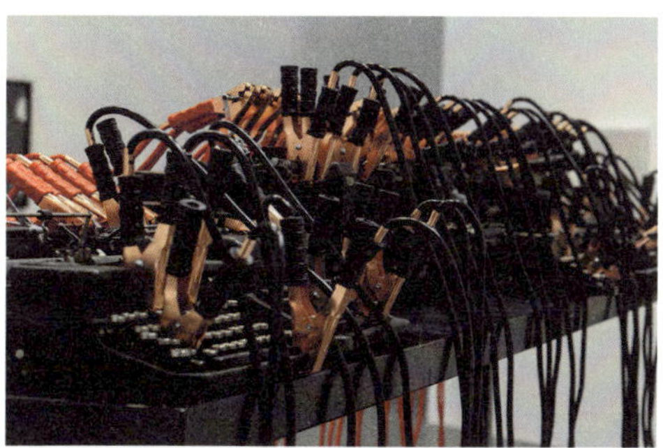
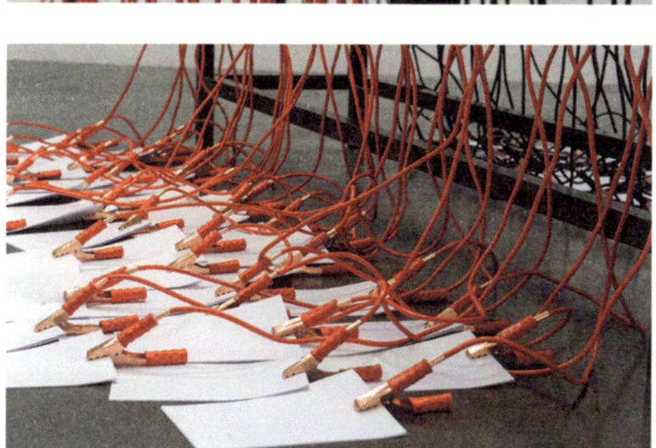
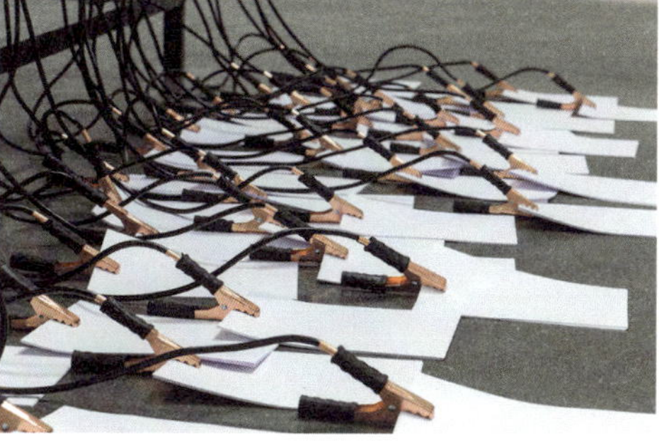

سعيد قمحاوي

(مواليد 1972،
المملكة العربية السعودية)
يقيم ويعمل في الرياض
(المملكة العربية السعودية)

سعيد قمحاوي رسامٌ وفنان مفاهيمي يتناول في عمله التراث الثقافي المحلي والقضايا الاجتماعية، وبعد تخرجه من معهد التربية الفنية بالرياض عام 1991، قام بتدريس الفن في المدارس الحكومية بجدة لأكثر من خمسة وعشرين عاماً، وهو عضو في بيت الفنانين بجدة والجمعية العربية السعودية للثقافة والفنون، كما شارك في تأسيس مركز تسامي للفنون البصرية عام 2014، وأسس استوديو رصيف في الرياض عام 2017؛ يتعمق سعيد في أعماله المفاهيمية المتعددة الطبقات في رصد القيم الاجتماعية والاختلافات الثقافية، ويستخدم مختلف المواد والوسائط لاستكشاف التفاعل المعقد بين التراث الثقافي والمعتقدات الدينية والوقائع المتغيرة في المجتمع المعاصر، ويلفت الانتباه بإبرازه القضايا المجتمعية إلى أهمية حماية التقاليد الثقافية مع الإقرار بضرورة التغيير والنمو المستمر.

شارك سعيد في العديد من المعارض الجماعية، ومن أبرزها معرض "من الأرض" في إثراء بالظهران، المملكة العربية السعودية (2023)؛ "تأثير التأمل" في حافظ غاليري بالرياض، المملكة العربية السعودية (2024)؛ "نور الرياض" في الرياض، المملكة العربية السعودية (2020)؛ "إضاءات: مختارات من معرض نور الرياض" في حي جميل بجدة، المملكة العربية السعودية (2021)؛ "العودة إلى الوطن" في أثر غاليري بجدة، المملكة العربية السعودية (2021)؛ "العبور"، فن جدة 21,39، المملكة العربية السعودية (2019)؛ "من الصحراء إلى الدلتا: الفن المعاصر في ممفيس" في جامعة ممفيس، الولايات المتحدة الأمريكية (2017)؛

"تدفق" في حافظ غاليري بالرياض، المملكة العربية السعودية (2017)؛ معرض أبوظبي للفنون في ويرهاوس 421 بأبوظبي، الإمارات العربية المتحدة (2017)؛ "الأرض وما بعد ذلك"، فن جدة 21,39، المملكة العربية السعودية (2016). وعرض أعماله دولياً، بما في ذلك في إيطاليا ومصر وسوريا وهولندا. وأقام معرضين فرديين في أتيلييه جدة، المملكة العربية السعودية (1998، 2002).

دخلت أعماله إلى المجموعات الفنية لعدد من المؤسسات السعودية، من أبرزها متحف عبد الرؤوف خليل في جدة بالمملكة العربية السعودية والرئاسة العامة لرعاية الشباب في المملكة العربية السعودية.

SAEED GAMHAWI

(b.1972, Saudi Arabia)
Lives and works in Riyadh,
Saudi Arabia

Saeed Gamhawi is a painter and a conceptual artist whose work tackles local cultural heritage and social issues. After graduating from the Institute of Art Education in Riyadh in 1991, he taught art in Jeddah public schools for more than twenty-five years. He is a member of the House of Artists in Jeddah and the Saudi Arabian Society for Culture and Arts. He also cofounded the Tasami Center for Visual Art in 2014, and he established Raseef Studio in Riyadh in 2017. Through his layered conceptual works, the artist delves into observations of social values and cultural differences. Employing various materials and mediums, Gamhawi explores the complex interplay between cultural heritage, religious beliefs, and the evolving realities of contemporary society. By foregrounding pertinent societal issues, he draws attention to the importance of protecting cultural traditions while also embracing the necessity of constant change and growth.

The artist has participated in several group exhibitions, including *From Earth*, Ithra, Dhahran, Saudi Arabia (2023); *Contemplation Effect*, Hafez Gallery, Riyadh, Saudi Arabia (2024); Noor Riyadh, Riyadh, Saudi Arabia (2020); *Illuminate: A Noor Riyadh Capsule*, Hayy Jameel, Jeddah, Saudi Arabia (2021); *Going Back Home*, ATHR Gallery, Jeddah, Saudi Arabia (2021); *Al Obour*, 21, 39 Jeddah Arts, Saudi Arabia (2019); *Desert to Delta: Contemporary Art in Memphis*, University of Memphis, USA (2017); *Flow*, Hafez Gallery, Riyadh, Saudi Arabia (2017); Abu Dhabi Art Fair, Warehouse421, Abu Dhabi, UAE (2017); and *Earth and Ever After*, 21, 39 Jeddah Arts, Saudi Arabia (2016). He has exhibited internationally, including in Italy, Egypt, Syria, and the Netherlands. He held solo exhibitions at Atelier Jeddah, Saudi Arabia (1998, 2002).

His work has been collected by several Saudi Arabian institutions, including the Abdul Raouf Khalil Museum, Jeddah, Saudi Arabia, and the General Presidency of Youth Welfare, Saudi Arabia.

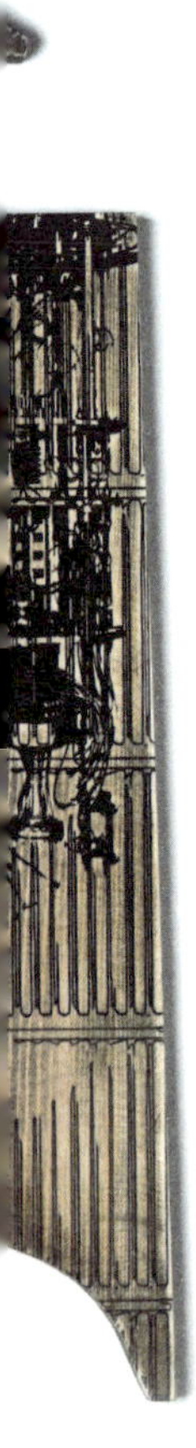

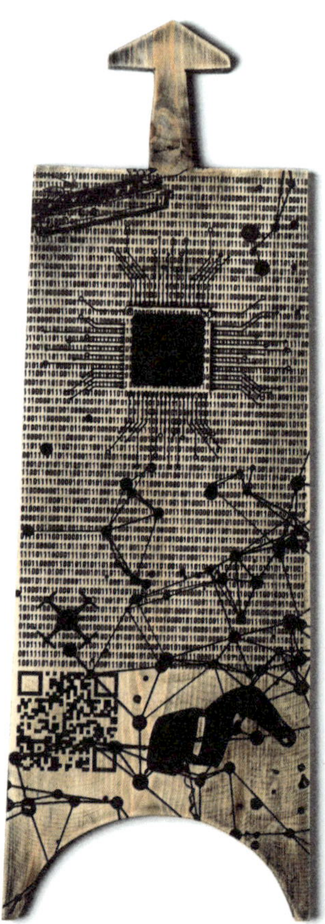

SAEED GAMHAWI
(b.1972, Saudi Arabia)

Engraved, 2024

Treated natural wood,
Charcoal with Arabic glue and laser engraving
72 × 24 cm
Courtesy of the artist

سعيد قمحاوي
(مواليد 1972، المملكة العربية السعودية)

محفور، 2024

خشب طبيعي معالج
وفحم مع صمغ عربي وحفر ليزر
72 × 24 سم
بإذن من الفنان

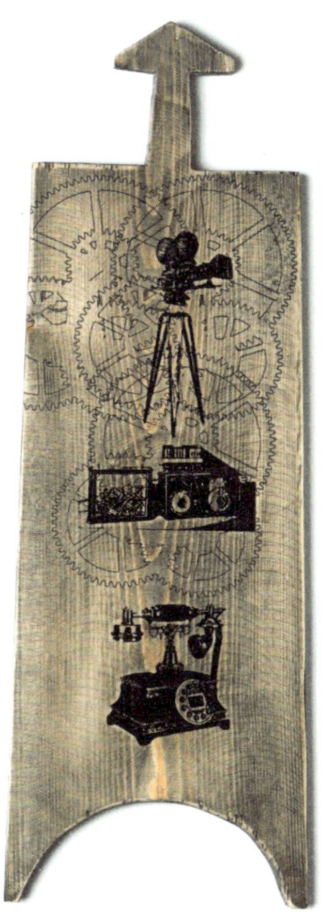
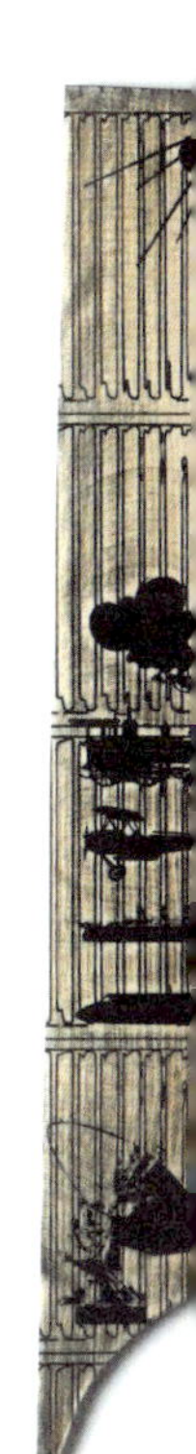

سامية حلبي

(مواليد 1936، فلسطين)
تقيم وتعمل في نيويورك
(الولايات المتحدة الأمريكية)

سامية حلبي مفكرةٌ ومعلمة وناشطة ورسامة تستلهم أعمالها من الطبيعة والتيارات التاريخية كالعمارة الإسلامية المبكرة والحركة الطليعية السوفييتية، نزحت سامية من فلسطين مع عائلتها عام 1948، وتلقت تعليمها في الغرب الأوسط الأمريكي، وحصلت على درجة البكالوريوس في التصميم من جامعة سينسيناتي، أوهايو (1959)؛ وماجستير في الرسم من جامعة ولاية ميشيغان، آن أربور (1960)، وماجستير في الفنون الجميلة في الرسم من جامعة إنديانا بلومنجتون (1963)، ونشرت العديد من الكتابات حول تاريخ الفن والتربية وعلم الجمال، وألّفت كتابَي "رسم مذبحة كفر قاسم" (2017) و"الأشكال المتنامية: رؤى جمالية لرسام تجريدي" (2017)، وكانت أول امرأة أستاذة مشاركة متفرّغة في كلية ييل للفنون (1973-1982)، وأدخلت برنامجاً للاحتراف الفني في المؤسسات الجامعية في جميع أنحاء الغرب الأوسط الأمريكي، وكانت أستاذة زائرة في جامعتي جنوب فلوريدا (1990) وهاواي (1966)، واعتقاداً منها بأن مقاربات الرسم الجديدة يمكن أن تحدث تحوّلاً في الرؤية والتفكير، انكبت على التجريب في الرسم والطباعة والفن الحركي المعتمد على الكمبيوتر والرسم المتحرّر من إطار اللوحة.

عُرضت أعمالها في مختلف أنحاء العالم، فقد شاركت في العديد من المعارض الجماعية، من أبرزها: "عقد السبعينيات: تسع نساء والتجريد" في غاليري زوركر بنيويورك، الولايات المتحدة الأمريكية (2017)؛ و"أبعاد مضيئة: مختارات من مجموعة غوغنهايم أبوظبي الفنية" في غوغنهايم أبوظبي، الإمارات العربية المتحدة (2014)؛ و"الجزيرة العربية المعاصرة" في غاليري أيام جدة، المملكة

العربية السعودية (2014)؛ و"جمع المؤنث" في غاليري آريا بباريس، فرنسا (2009)؛ و"فلسطين: الإبداع في جميع حالاته" في معهد العالم العربي بباريس، فرنسا (2009)؛ و"مرققن ومعالَج" في مركز سانغري دي كريستو للفنون، بويبلو، الولايات المتحدة الأمريكية (1991)؛ وبينالي هافانا الثالث، كوبا (1989)؛ و"أحدث المقتنيات" في غوغنهايم نيويورك، الولايات المتحدة الأمريكية (1975). وتشمل معارضها الفردية "العتامة والشفافية" في غاليري أيام ببيروت، لبنان (2018)؛ و"الرسومات التوثيقية لمذبحة كفر قاسم" في متحف جامعة بيرزيت بالضفة الغربية، فلسطين (2017)؛ و"لوحة من الستينيات والسبعينيات" في غاليري أيام بلندن، المملكة المتحدة (2015)؛ و"لغة بديعة نافعة: أعمال سامية حلبي" في مكتبة مقاطعة تومبكينز العامة، إيثاكا، نيويورك، الولايات المتحدة الأمريكية (2006)؛ و"لون فلسطين (إيقاعات من فلسطين)" في متحف شاتو دوفرين بمونتريال، كندا (2001)؛ و"قوى التغيير" في المتحف الوطني للمرأة بواشنطن العاصمة، الولايات المتحدة الأمريكية (1994)؛ و"فنانون فلسطينيون" في دار الفنانين بأوسلو، النرويج (1981).

دخلت أعمالها إلى العديد من المجموعات الفنية العامة والخاصة، من أبرزها غوغنهايم نيويورك، الولايات المتحدة الأمريكية؛ وغوغنهايم أبوظبي، الإمارات العربية المتحدة؛ ومتحف كليفلاند للفنون، الولايات المتحدة الأمريكية؛ ومعهد العالم العربي بباريس، فرنسا؛ ومعهد شيكاغو للفنون، الولايات المتحدة الأمريكية؛ ومؤسسة برجيل للفنون بالشارقة، الإمارات العربية المتحدة؛ ومؤسسة دلول للفنون ببيروت، لبنان؛ ودارة الفنون - مؤسسة خالد شومان بعمّان، الأردن؛ وجامعة بيرزيت برام الله، فلسطين.

SAMIA HALABY

(b. 1936, Palestine)
Lives and works in New York, USA

Samia Halaby is a thinker, educator, activist, and painter who draws inspiration from nature and historical movements, such as early Islamic architecture and the Soviet avant-garde. Displaced from Palestine with her family in 1948, she was educated in the American Midwest. She received a bachelor's degree in design from the University of Cincinnati, Ohio (1959); a master's in painting from Michigan State University, Ann Arbor (1960); and an MFA in painting from Indiana University, Bloomington (1963). The artist has published numerous writings on art history, pedagogy, and aesthetics. She also authored *Drawing the Kafr Qasem Massacre* (2017) and *Growing Shapes: Aesthetic Insights of an Abstract Painter* (2017). In addition, Halaby was the first full-time female associate professor at the Yale School of Art (1973–1982), introduced an undergraduate studio art program to institutions throughout the American Midwest, and was a visiting professor at the University of South Florida (1990) and the University of Hawaii (1966). Believing that new approaches to painting can transform our ways of seeing and thinking, she often experiments in drawing, printmaking, computer-based kinetic art, and free-from-the-stretcher painting.

Halaby's work has been exhibited extensively around the world. Select group exhibitions include *1970s: Nine Women and Abstraction*, Zürcher Gallery, New York, USA (2017); *Seeing through Light: Selections from the Guggenheim Abu Dhabi Collection*, Guggenheim Abu Dhabi, UAE (2014); *Contemporary Arabia*, Ayyam Gallery Jeddah, Saudi Arabia (2014); *Féminin Pluriel*, Area Gallery, Paris, France (2009); *Palestine: La création dans tous ses états*, Institut du monde arabe, Paris, France (2009); *Digitized and Manipulated*, Sangre De Cristo Arts Center, Pueblo, USA (1991); Tercero Bienal de la Habana, Havana, Cuba (1989); and *Recent Acquisitions*, Guggenheim New York, USA (1975). Select solo exhibitions include *Opacity and Transparency*, Ayyam Gallery, Beirut, Lebanon (2018); *Documentary Drawings of the Kafr Qasem Massacre*, Birzeit University Museum, West Bank, Palestine (2017); *Painting from the Sixties and Seventies*, Ayyam Gallery, London, UK (2015); *A Useful Magnificent Language: The Work of Samia A. Halaby*, Tompkins County Public Library, Ithaca, NY, USA (2006); *Couleur Palestine (Rhythms from Palestine)*, Le musée du Château Dufresne, Montreal, Canada (2001); *Forces of Change*, National Museum of Women, Washington D.C., USA (1994); and *Palestinske Kunstnere (Palestinian Artists)*, Kunstnernes Hus, Oslo, Norway (1981), among others.

The artist's work is included in numerous public and private collections, such as the Guggenheim New York, USA; the Guggenheim Abu Dhabi, UAE; the Cleveland Museum of Art, USA; the Institut du monde arabe, Paris, France; the Art Institute of Chicago, USA; the Barjeel Art Foundation, Sharjah, UAE; the Dalloul Art Foundation, Beirut, Lebanon; Darat al Funun—The Khalid Shoman Foundation, Amman, Jordan; and Birzeit University, Ramallah, Palestine.

لوحـة حركية ميرمجة على كمبيوتر أميغا وصوت
دقيقتان و30 ثانية
خمس نسخ + نسختان فنيتان
بإذن من الفنانة وغاليري صفير زملر
في بيروت وهامبورغ

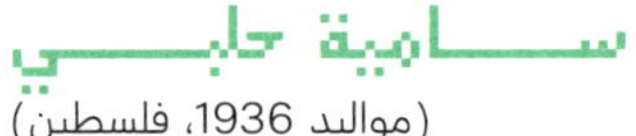

سامية حلبي

(مواليد 1936، فلسطين)

بنائي 10، 1986

SAMIA HALABY

(b. 1936, Palestine)

Constructivist 10, 1986

Kinetic painting coded on an Amiga computer and sound
2 min., 30 sec.
Ed. 5 + 2 AP
Courtesy of the artist and Sfeir-Semler Gallery,
Beirut and Hamburg

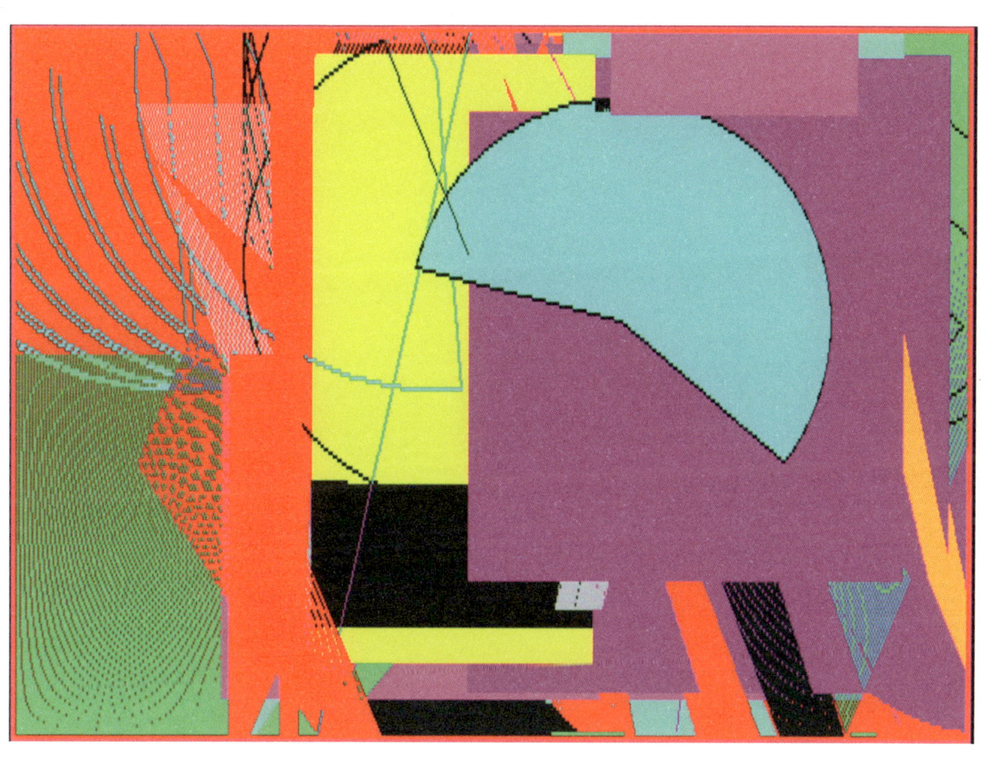

SAMIA HALABY

(b. 1936, Palestine)

Dark Weaver, 1987

Kinetic painting coded on an Amiga computer and sound
17 sec.
Ed. 5 + 2 AP
Courtesy of the artist and Sfeir-Semler Gallery,
Beirut and Hamburg

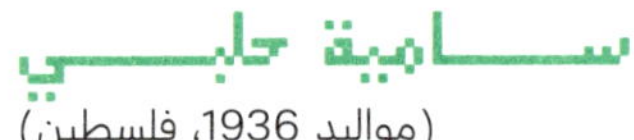

(مواليد 1936، فلسطين)

الحائلُ الغامض، 1987

لوحـة حركية مبرمجة على كمبيوتر أميغا وصوت
17 ثانية
خمس نسخ + نسختان فنيتان
بإذن من الفنانة وغاليري صفير زملر
في بيروت وهامبورغ

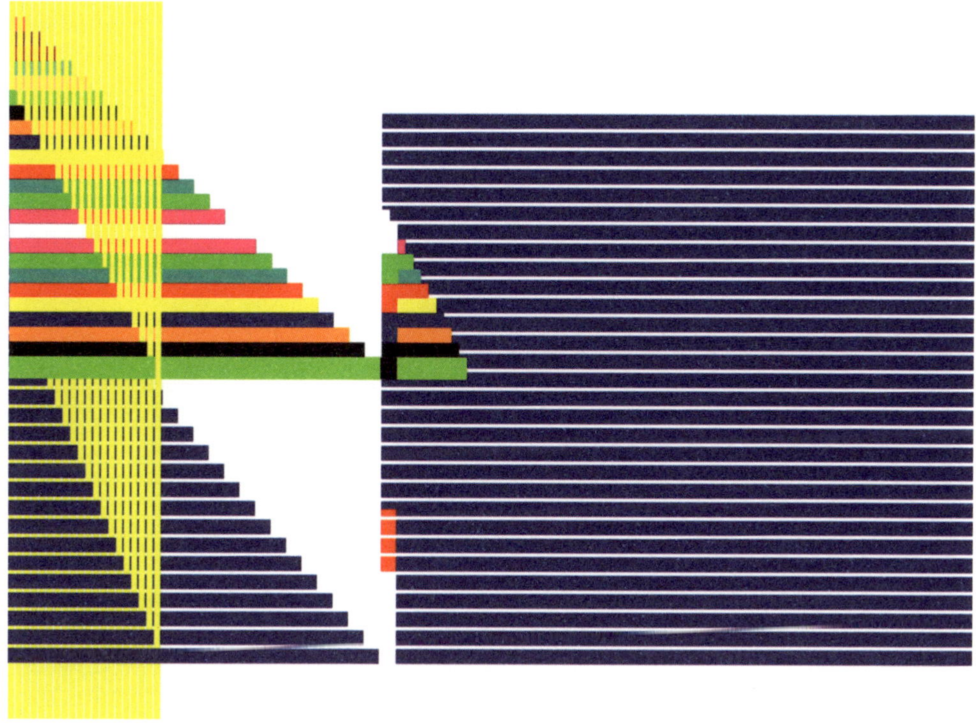

سامية حلبي

(مواليد 1936، فلسطين)

رقصة 3، 1988

لوحـة حركية مبرمجة على كمبيوتر أميغا وصوت
دقيقة و36 ثانية
خمس نسخ + نسختان فنيتان
بإذن من الفنانة وغاليري صفير زملر
في بيروت وهامبورغ

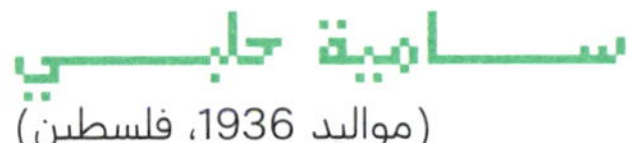

SAMIA HALABY

(b. 1936, Palestine)

Dance 3, 1988

Kinetic painting coded on an Amiga computer and sound
1 min., 36 sec.
Ed. 5 + 2 AP
Courtesy of the artist and Sfeir-Semler Gallery,
Beirut and Hamburg

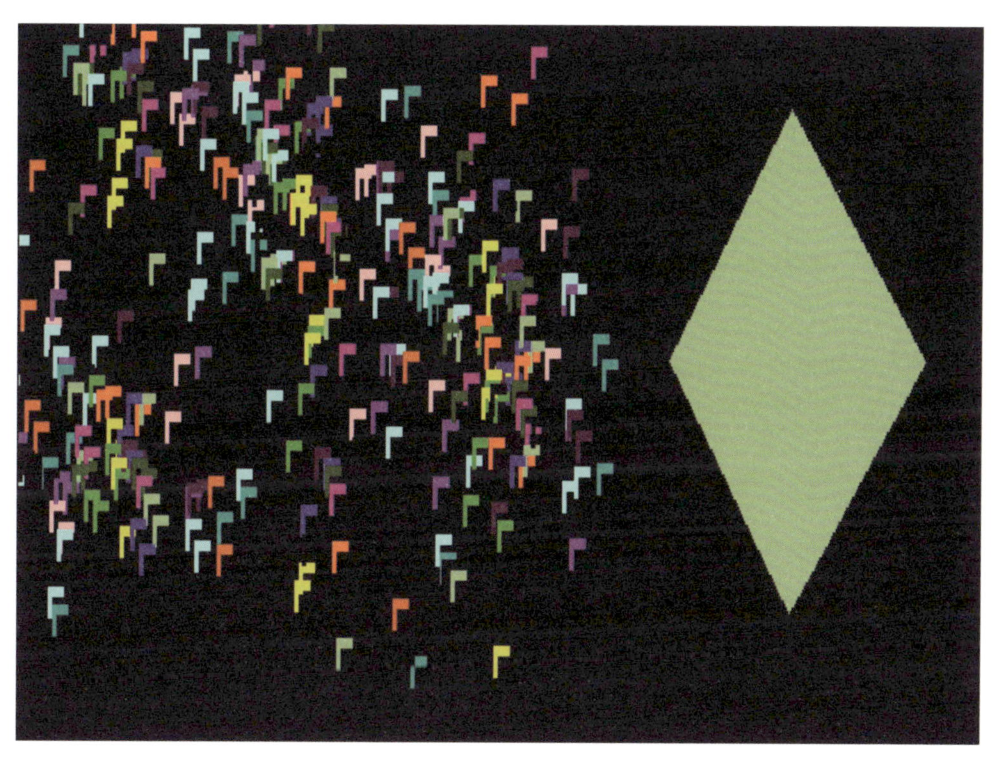

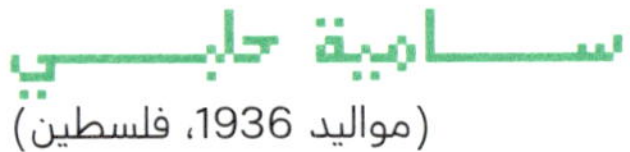

SAMIA HALABY

(b. 1936, Palestine)

DUP, 1988

Kinetic painting coded on an Amiga computer and sound
1 min., 36 sec.
Ed. 5 + 2 AP
Courtesy of the artist and Sfeir-Semler Gallery,
Beirut and Hamburg

سامية حلبي
(مواليد 1936، فلسطين)

1988 ،*DUP*

لوحـة حركية مبرمجة على كمبيوتر أميغا وصوت
39 ثانية
خمس نسخ + نسختان فنيتان
بإذن من الفنانة وغاليري صفير زملر
في بيروت وهامبورغ

(مواليـد 1937، المملكـة المتحـدة)
يقيـم ويعمـل بيـن لنـدن
(المملكـة المتحـدة)
ونورمانـدي (فرنسـا)

ديفيـد هوكنـي هو رسامٌ وطبّـاع ومصـور ومصمم مسـرحي للأوبـرا والباليـه، كان لـه إسـهام كبيـر في حركـة فـن البـوب في السـتينيات مـن القرن العشـرين، ويُعتبـر أحـد أكثـر الفنانيـن البريطانييـن تأثيـراً فـي القرنيـن العشـرين والحـادي والعشـرين، درس الفن في كليـة برادفورد بالمملكـة المتحـدة (1953-1957) والكليـة الملكيـة للفنـون بلنـدن بالمملكـة المتحـدة (1959-1962)، ثـم قـام بالتدريـس فـي الولايـات المتحـدة فـي جامعـات أيـوا وكولـورادو وكاليفورنيا (لـوس أنجلـوس) وجامعـة كاليفورنيـا فـي بيركلـي؛ تركّـز موضوعاتـه فـي المقـام الأول علـى سـيرة حياتـه، بما فـي ذلـك البورتريهـات والبورتريهـات الذاتيـة، إلى جانـب المشـاهد الغَرضيـة الهادئـة لأصدقائـه ومسـكنه، خلال التسـعينيات مـن القرن العشـرين، جرب العمل علـى المناظـر الطبيعيـة التجريديـة بينمـا كان يتابـع الاهتمام بالتكنولوجيـات الجديـدة، ونشـر العديد من الكتب المصورة بما فيها رسـوم "سـت حكايات خيالية للأخويـن غريـم" (1970) و"القيثارة الزرقاء" (1977).

شـارك فـي أكثـر مـن 500 معـرض جماعـي، ومـن أبرزهـا؛ بينالـي ويتنـي في متحـف ويتني للفن الأمريكـي بنيويـورك، الولايـات المتحـدة الأمريكيـة (2004)، وبينالي سـاو باولو، البرازيل (1989). كما أقـام أكثـر مـن 400 معـرض فـردي، تتضمـن "ديفيـد هوكنـي: أكبـر وأقـرب (وليـس أصغـر وأبعـد)" فـي غاليري لايـت روم سـيول، كوريـا الجنوبية (2024)؛ "ديفيـد هوكنـي: عكـس المنظـور، مطبوعـات مـن مجموعـة جوردان شـنيتزر ومؤسسـته العائليـة" في متحـف هونولولـو للفنـون، هـاواي (2023)؛ و"عيـن هوكنـي: فـن وتكنولوجيـا التصويـر" فـي متحـف فيتزويليـام بكامبريـدج، المملكـة المتحـدة (2022)؛

"ديفيد هوكنـي" في تيـت بريطانيا بلنـدن، المملكة المتحـدة (2017)؛ "ديفيـد هوكنـي: معـرض أكبر" فـي متحف دي يونـغ بسـان فرانسيسـكو، الولايات المتحـدة الأمريكيـة (2013)؛ و"صـورة أكبـر" فـي غوغنهايـم بلبـاو، إسـبانيا (2012)؛ و"ديفيد هوكنـي: الطبيعـة وحسـب" فـي قاعـة وورث للفنـون فـي شفابيـش هال، ألمانيا (2009)؛ و"بورتريهات ديفيـد هوكنـي" في القاعة الوطنية للبورتريه بلنـدن، المملكـة المتحـدة (2006)؛ متحف مقاطعة لوس أنجلوس للفنـون بلوس أنجلـوس، الولايات المتحدة الأمريكيـة (1988)؛ و"لوحات ومطبوعات ورسـومات 1960-1970" فـي غاليـري وايـت تشـابل بلنـدن، المملكـة المتحـدة (1970).

تحتفظ غالـيري 1853 بالعديد من أعماله في سـالتس ميل (سـالتير، المملكة المتحدة) بالقرب من مسـقط رأسـه في برادفورد، وتحتفظ مؤسسة ديفيد هوكنـي بمجموعـة كبيـرة أخـرى مـن الأعمال، في حين دخلـت أعمال أخـرى إلى العديـد مـن المجموعات الفنيـة العامـة والخاصـة في جميـع أنحـاء العالم، مـن أبرزهـا مجموعـة متحـف متروبوليتـان للفنون بنيويـورك، الولايـات المتحـدة الأمريكيـة؛ ومتحف الفـن الحديـث بنيويـورك، الولايـات المتحـدة الأمريكيـة؛ ومركـز بومبيدو بباريـس، فرنسـا؛ ومتحف سـميثسـونيان للفـن الأمريكـي بواشـنطن العاصمة، الولايـات المتحـدة الأمريكيـة؛ ومتحف الفن المعاصر طوكيـو، اليابان؛ ومتحف الفنون الجميلة ببوسـطن، الولايـات المتحـدة الأمريكيـة؛ وتيت مـودرن بلندن، المملكـة المتحـدة؛ ومتحـف مقاطعـة لوس أنجلـوس للفنـون، الولايـات المتحـدة الأمريكيـة؛ ومتحـف هونولولـو للفنـون، الولايات المتحـدة الأمريكية.

DAVID HOCKNEY

(b. 1937, UK)
Lives and works between
London, UK,
and Normandy, France

David Hockney is a painter, draftsman, printmaker, photographer, and stage designer for opera and ballet. An important contributor to the Pop art movement of the 1960s, he is considered to be one of the most influential British artists of the twentieth and twenty-first centuries. He studied art at Bradford College, UK (1953–1957), and the Royal College of Art, London, UK (1959–1962). He then taught in the USA at the University of Iowa, the University of Colorado, the University of California, Los Angeles, and the University of California, Berkeley. Hockney's subject matter is primarily autobiographical, including portraits and self-portraits, along with quiet, incidental scenes of his friends as well as his quarters. During the 1990s, the artist experimented with abstract landscapes while pursuing a long-standing interest in new technologies. He published several series of graphic works in book form, including illustrations for *Six Fairy Tales from the Brothers Grimm* (1970) and *The Blue Guitar* (1977).

Hockney has been featured in more than five hundred group exhibitions, including the Whitney Biennial, Whitney Museum of American Art, New York, USA (2004), and the São Paulo Biennial, Brazil (1989), among many others. He has also held more than four hundred solo exhibitions, including *David Hockney: Bigger & Closer (not smaller & further away)*, Lightroom Seoul, South Korea (2024); *David Hockney: Perspective Should Be Reversed, Prints from the Collections of Jordan D. Schnitzer and His Family Foundation*, Honolulu Museum of Art, Hawaii (2023); *Hockney's Eye: The Art and Technology of Depiction*, Fitzwilliam Museum, Cambridge, UK (2022); *David Hockney*, Tate Britain, London, UK (2017); *David Hockney: A Bigger Exhibition*, de Young Museum, San Francisco, USA (2013); *A Bigger Picture*, Guggenheim Bilbao, Spain (2012); *David Hockney: Just Nature*, Kunsthalle Würth, Schwäbisch Hall, Germany (2009); *David Hockney Portraits*, National Portrait Gallery, London, UK (2006); LACMA, Los Angeles, USA (1988); and *Paintings, Prints and Drawings 1960–1970*, Whitechapel Gallery, London, UK (1970).

Many of the artist's works are housed in the 1853 Gallery at Salts Mill, Saltaire, UK, near his hometown of Bradford. Another large group is held by the David Hockney Foundation. His works are part of numerous public and private collections worldwide, such as the Metropolitan Museum of Art, New York, USA; the Museum of Modern Art, New York, USA; the Centre Pompidou, Paris, France; the Smithsonian American Art Museum, Washington, D.C., USA; the Museum of Contemporary Art Tokyo, Japan; the Museum of Fine Arts, Boston, USA; Tate Modern, London, UK; the Los Angeles County Museum of Art, USA; and the Honolulu Museum of Art, USA.

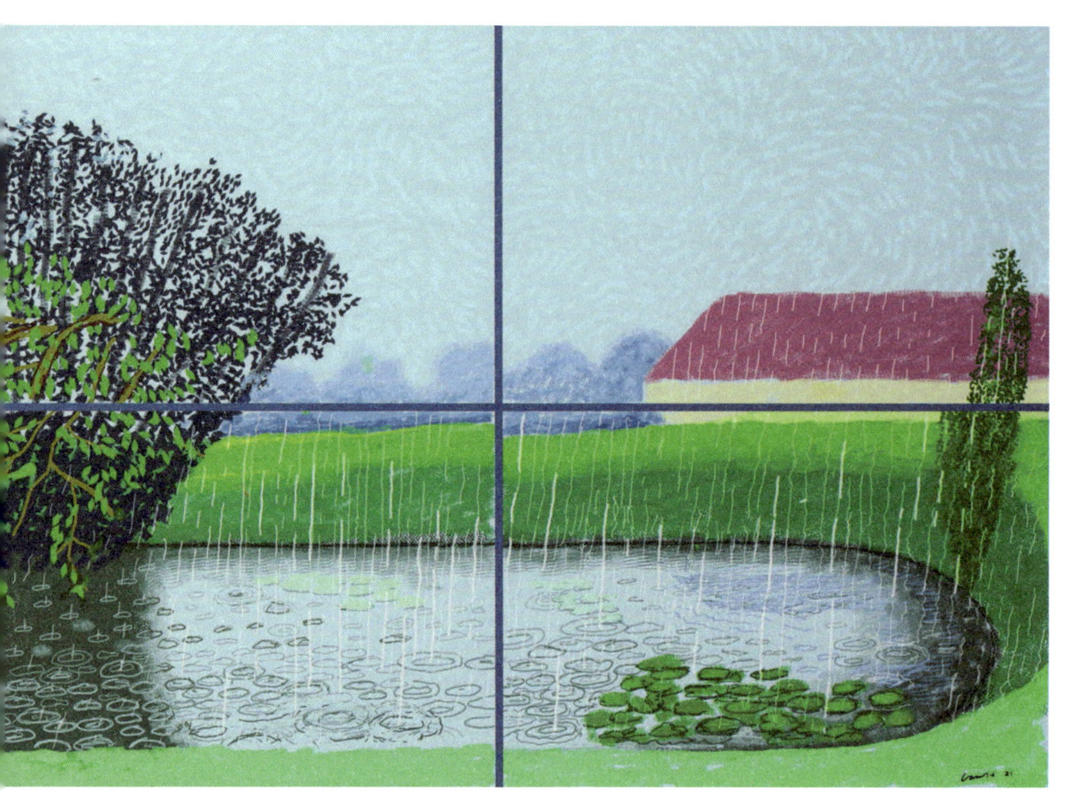

ديفيـــد هوكنــي

(مواليد 1937، المملكة المتحدة)

25 يوليو - 7 أغسطس 2021،
المطر المنهمر على البركة، 2021

عمـل واحد مؤلف من ثماني لوحات على جهاز iPad، مطبوع
علـى ورق، مثبت على ألواح دييوند من الألمنيوم
281.9 × 99.7 سم
بإذن من الفنان وغاليري بيس (Pace)

DAVID HOCKNEY

(b. 1937, UK)

25th July - 7th August 2021,
Rain on the Pond, 2021

Eight iPad paintings comprising a single work, printed on
paper, mounted on Dibond
99.7 × 281.9 cm
Courtesy of the artist and Pace Gallery

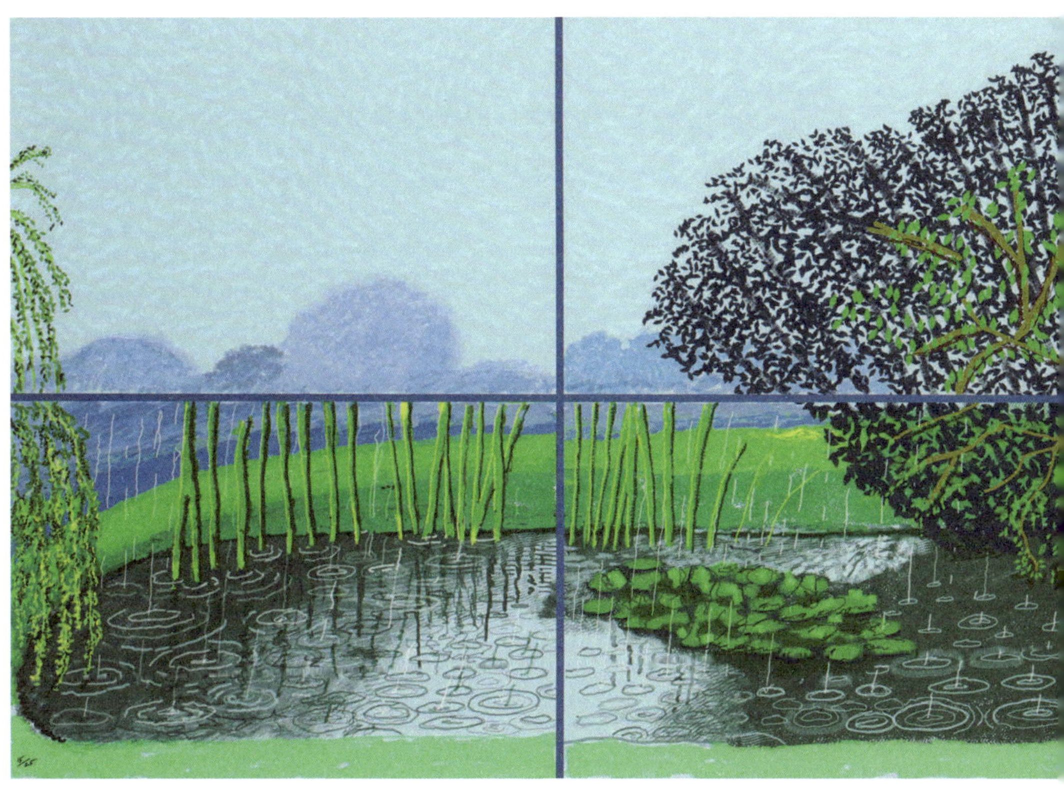

DAVID HOCKNEY

(b. 1937, UK)

Plug, 2011

iPad drawing printed on paper
94 × 71.1 cm
Courtesy of the artist and Pace Gallery

ديفيـــد هوكنــي
(مواليد 1937، المملكة المتحدة)

قابس كهربائي، 2011

رسم على جهاز iPad، مطبوع على ورق
94 × 71.1 سم
بإذن من الفنان وغاليري بيس (Pace)

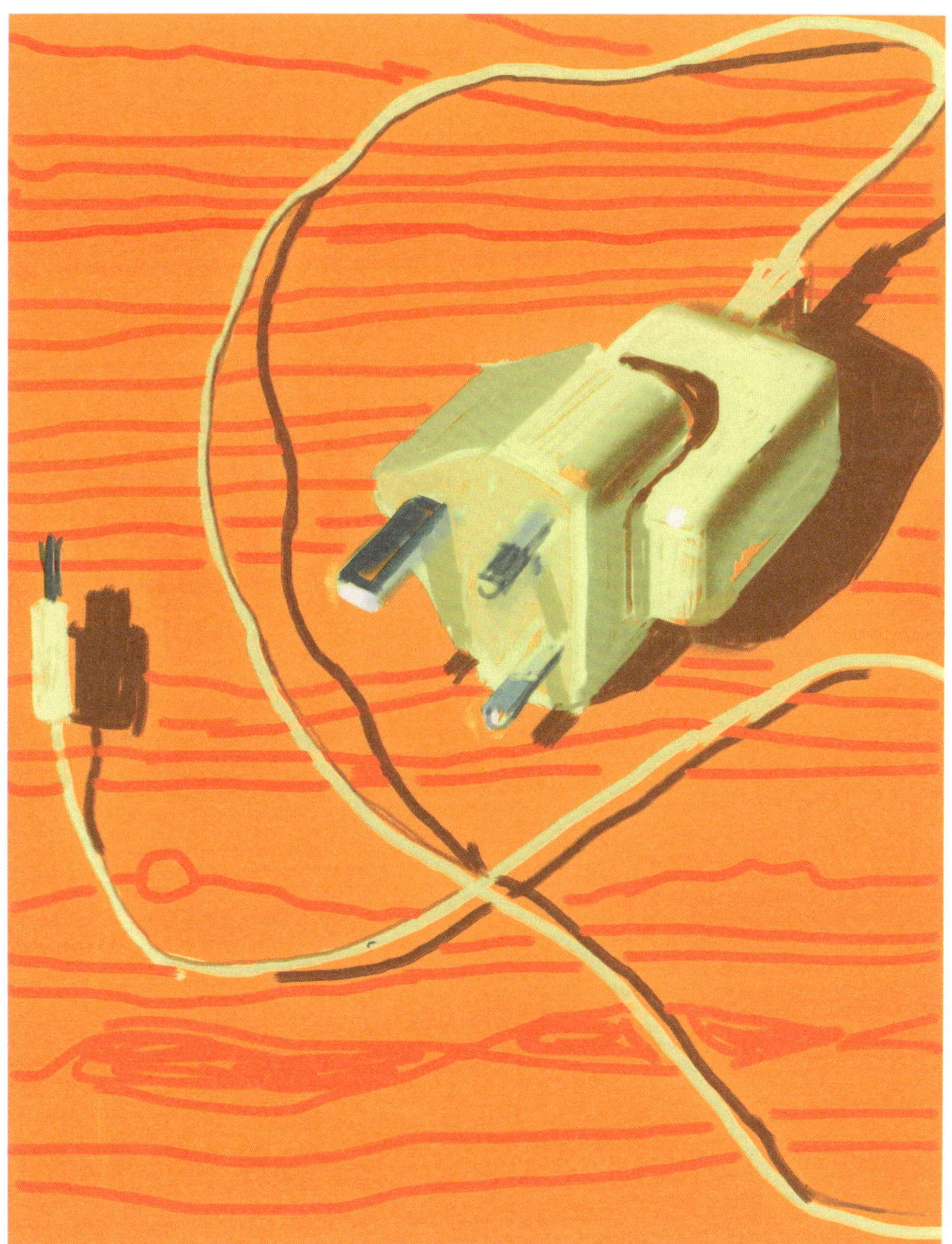

(مواليد 1937، المملكة المتحدة)

حلول الربيع في وولدغيت، شرق يوركشاير في عام 2011، - 25 فبراير، 2011

رسم على جهاز iPad، مطبوع على ورق
105.4 × 139.7 سم
بإذن من الفنان وغاليري بيس (Pace)

(b. 1937, UK)

The Arrival of Spring in Woldgate, East Yorkshire in 2011 (Twenty Eleven) - 25 February, 2011

iPad drawing printed on paper
139.7 × 105.4 cm
Courtesy of the artist and Pace Gallery

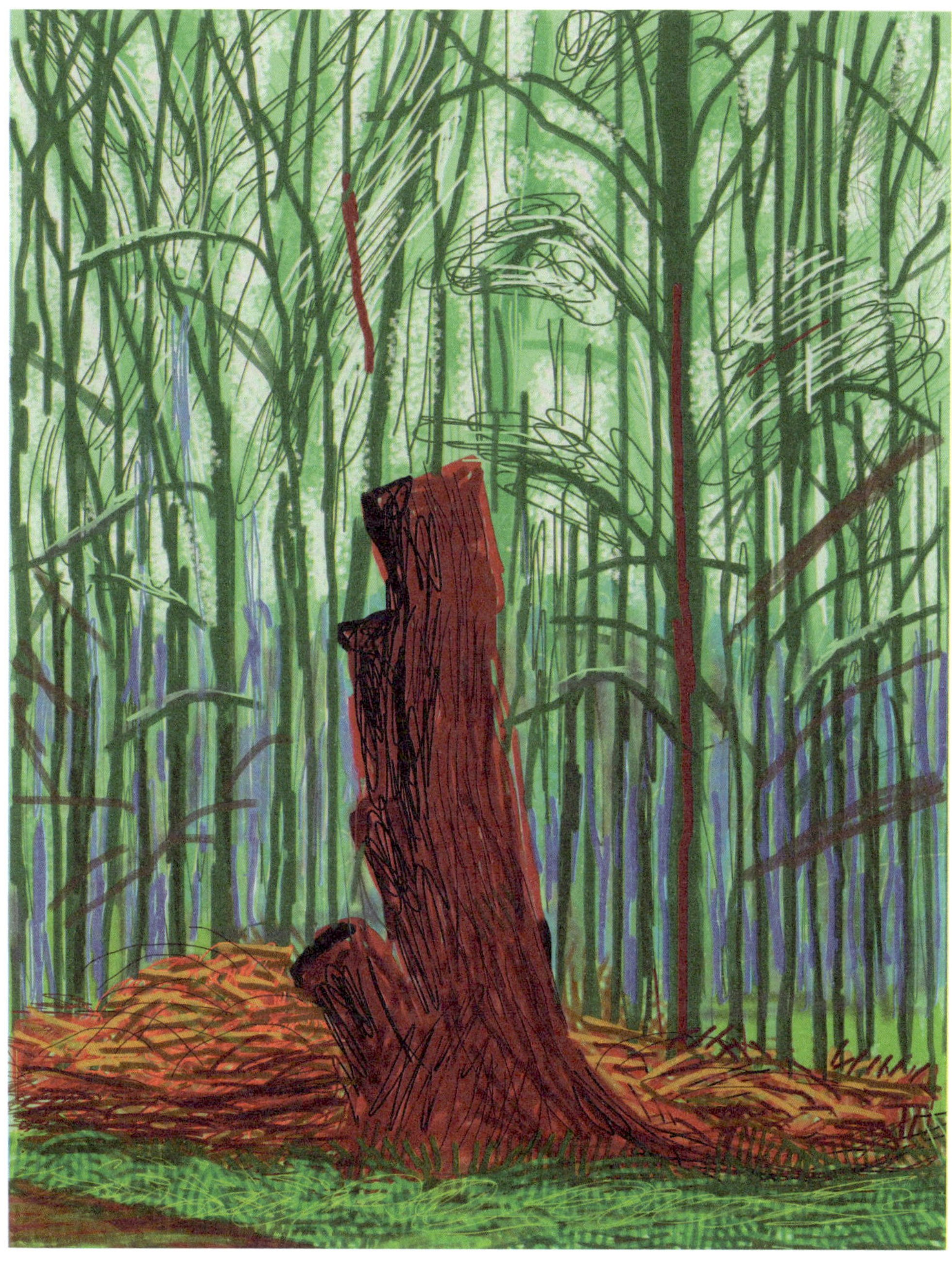

سفيان إدريسي

(مواليد 1986، المغرب)
يقيم ويعمل في الرباط (المغرب)

سفيان إدريسي فنانٌ مفاهيمي وشخصية بارزة في حركة ما بعد الإنترنت في المغرب، واستفاد من معرفته بالفن الجرافيكي وعلوم الكمبيوتر، وشارك إلى جانب محمد شرورو بتأسيس مجموعة رادار في عام 2009 والتي لعبت دوراً تاريخياً في الطليعة المغربية، من خلال تحويل الصور الأصلية الموجودة على الإنترنت إلى أعمال فنية، متبعة تقليد الفن الجاهز، ويدمج إدريسي في أعماله أدوات الذكاء الاصطناعي الجديدة التي ظهرت في القرن الحادي والعشرين.

شارك في العديد من المعارض الجماعية، ومن أبرزها؛ "رسم من المغرب، آآآه" في معرض باريس الدولي، فرنسا (2023)؛ "أحب إيف سان لوران" في مؤسسة إيف سان لوران بإيفورا، البرتغال (2022)؛ "في المملكة" في مرسى منطقة التصميم بميامي، الولايات المتحدة الأمريكية (2019)؛ "نور القرن"، بينالي غوانجو، كوريا الجنوبية (2015)؛ برنامج "غوغل آرت"، معرض جماعي على الإنترنت، سان فرانسيسكو، الولايات المتحدة الأمريكية (2013)؛ "مساترمايند 1" في غاليري فينيس كادر بالدار البيضاء (GVCC)، المغرب (2011). وتشمل معارضه الفردية معرض "مبني على الويب الجزء الأول" في غاليري فينيس كادر بالدار البيضاء (GVCC)، المغرب (2022)؛ "مبني على الويب الجزء الثاني" في غاليري فينيس كادر بالدار البيضاء (GVCC)، المغرب (2022)؛ "الرسم بالذكاء الاصطناعي" في غاليري فينيس كادر بالدار البيضاء (GVCC)، المغرب (2019)؛ "الرسم باستخدام html" في غاليري فينيس كادر بالدار البيضاء (GVCC)، المغرب (2012).

دخلت أعماله إلى العديد من المجموعات الفنية الخاصة والعامة، ومن أبرزها متحف محمد السادس للفن الحديث والمعاصر في الرباط، المغرب؛ ومؤسسة بارجيل للفنون في الشارقة، الإمارات العربية المتحدة؛ وR42 في سان فرانسيسكو، الولايات المتحدة الأمريكية؛ والمجموعة الوطنية الكورية.

SOUFIANE IDRISSI

(b. 1986, Morocco)
Lives and works in Rabat, Morocco

Soufiane Idrissi is a conceptual artist and prominent figure associated with the post-Internet movement in Morocco. Drawing from his background in graphic art and computer science, he cofounded the collective Radar in 2009, alongside Mohammed Chrouro. This group played a historic role in the Moroccan avant-garde, transforming original images found on the Internet into works of art, following the tradition of ready-made art. He incorporates the dimension of new, twenty-first-century artificial intelligence tools into his works.

The artist has participated in multiple group exhibitions, including *A Drawing for Morocco, Aaahhh!!!* Paris Internationale, France (2023); *Love Yves Saint Laurent*, Yves Saint Laurent Foundation, Evora, Portugal (2022); *In the Kingdom*, the Arsenale of Design District Space, Miami, USA (2019); *Light of Century*, Gwangju Biennale, South Korea (2015); *Google Art Program*, online collective exhibition, San Francisco, USA (2013); and *Mastermind 1*, GVCC Gallery, Casablanca, Morocco (2011), among others. Selected solo exhibitions include *The Web Based Part 1*, GVCC Gallery, Casablanca, Morocco (2022); *The Web Based Part 2*, GVCC Gallery, Casablanca, Morocco (2022); *Painting with Artificial Intelligence*, GVCC Gallery, Casablanca, Morocco (2019); and *Painting with html*, GVCC Gallery, Casablanca, Morocco (2012).

His works are in numerous private collections, as well as several public collections, including those of the Mohammed VI Museum of Modern and Contemporary Art, Rabat, Morocco; the Barjeel Art Foundation, Sharjah, UAE; R42 San Francisco, USA; and the National Collection of Korea, South Korea.

سـفيان إدريسـي
(مواليد 1986، المغرب)

تجريد مع الذكاء الاصطناعي 2، 2018

ألوان زيتية على قماش
180 × 140 سم
بإذن مــن الفنان وغاليري فينيس كادر في الدار البيضاء

SOUFIANE IDRISSI

(b. 1986, Morocco)

Abstract with AI 2, 2018

Oil on canvas
180 × 140 cm
Courtesy of the artist and GVCC Gallery, Casablanca

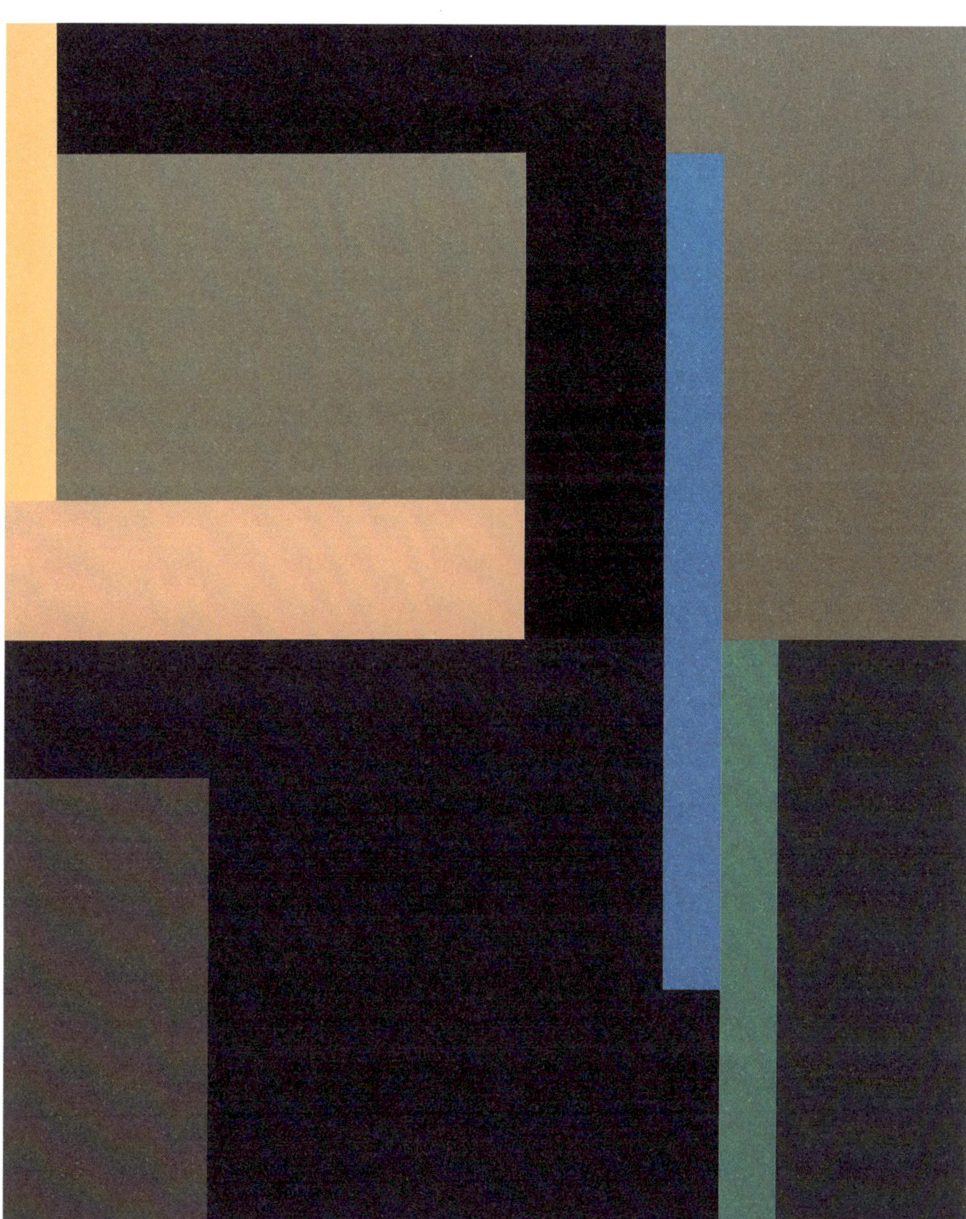

SOUFIANE IDRISSI

(b. 1986, Morocco)

Abstract with HTML 31, 2021

Oil on canvas
180 × 140 cm
Courtesy of the artist and GVCC Gallery, Casablanca

سـفيان إدريسي

(مواليد 1986، المغرب)

تجريد مع HTML 31، 2021

ألوان زيتية على قماش
180 × 140 سم
بإذن مـن الفنان وغاليري فينيس كادر في الدار البيضاء

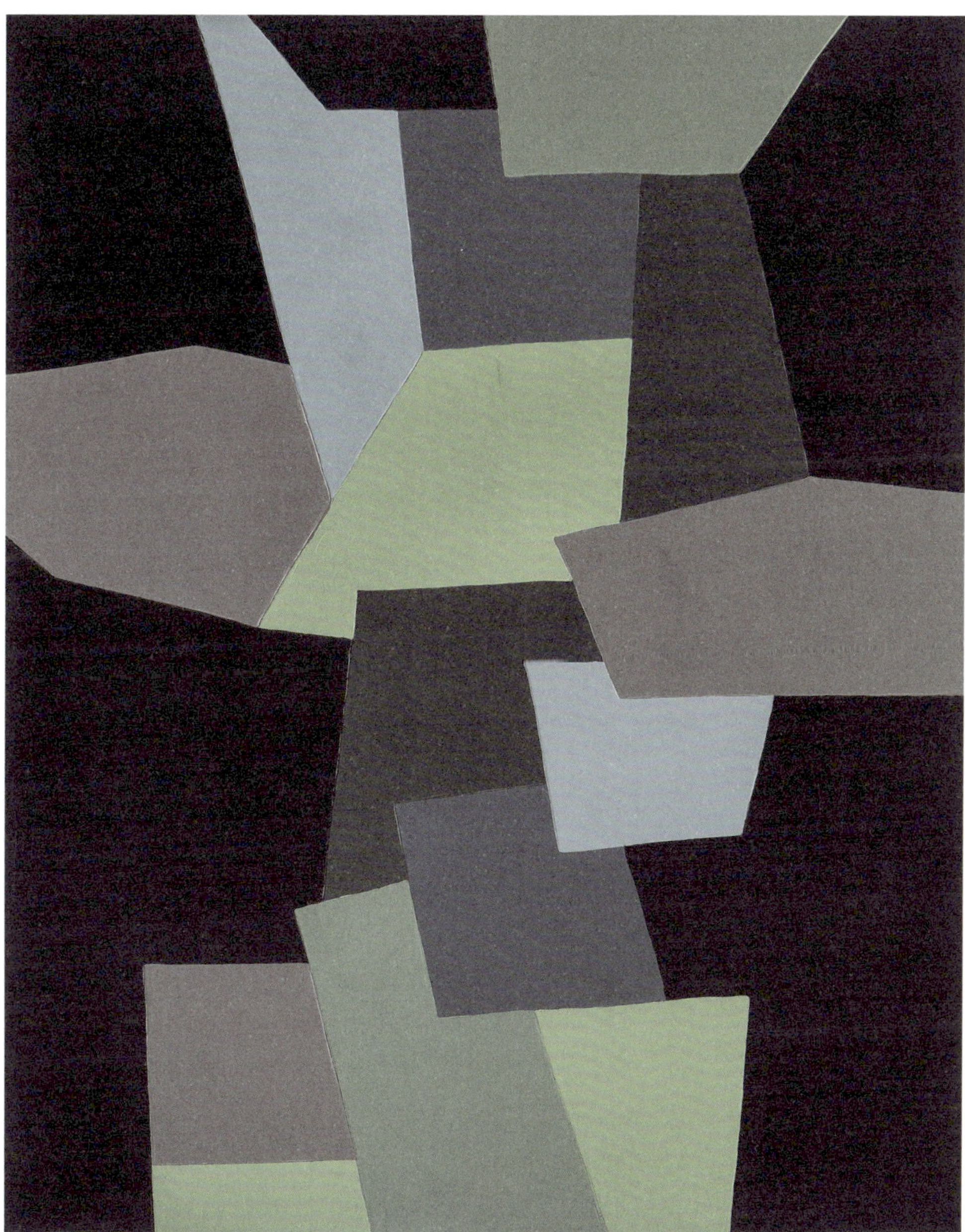

SOUFIANE IDRISSI
(b. 1986, Morocco)

Painting with Artificial Intelligence 21,
2016

Oil on canvas
180 × 140 cm
Courtesy of the artist and GVCC Gallery, Casablanca

سـفيان إدريسـي
(مواليد 1986، المغرب)

الرسم مع الذكاء الاصطناعي 21،
2016

ألوان زيتية على قماش
140 × 180 سم
بإذن مـن الفنان وغاليري فينيس كادر في الدار البيضاء

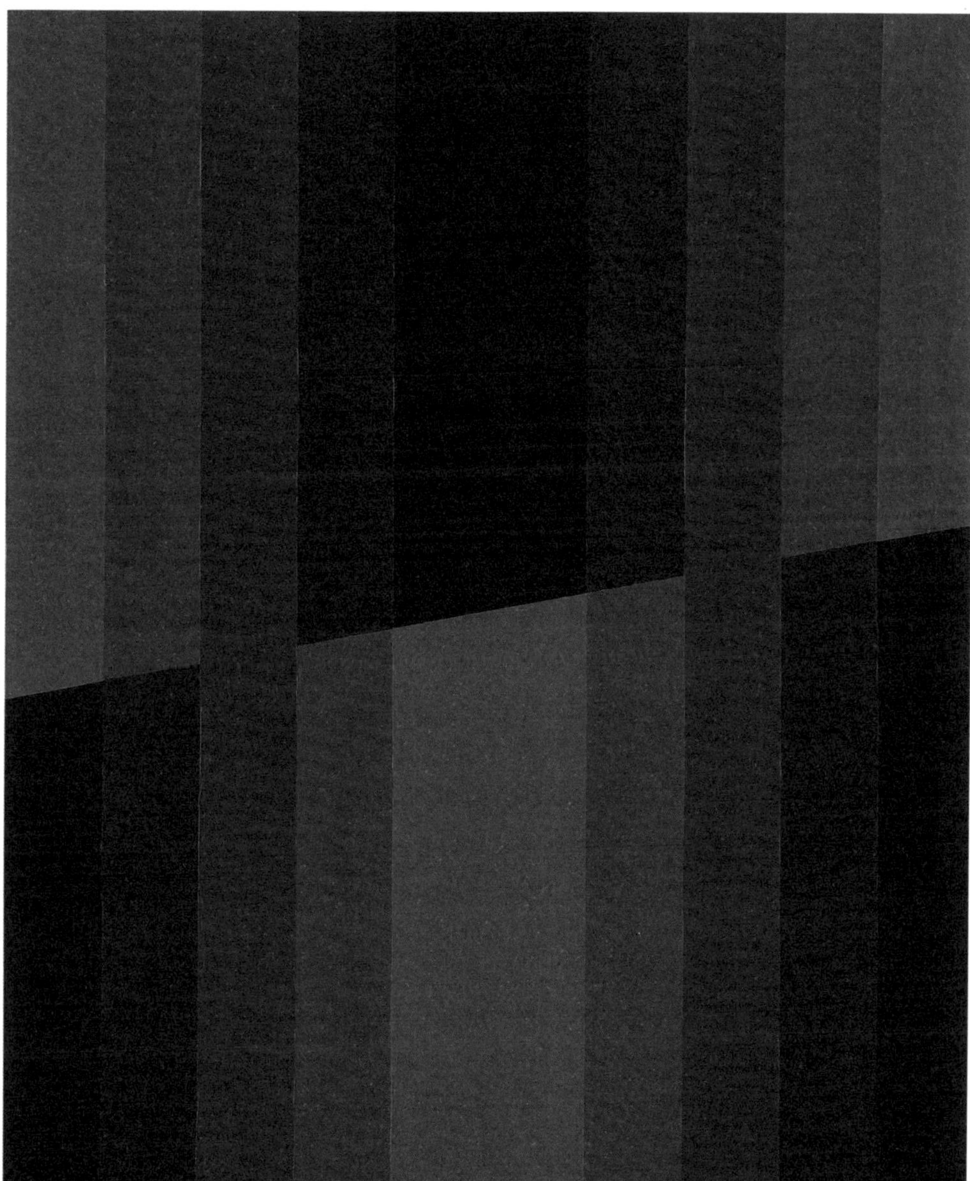

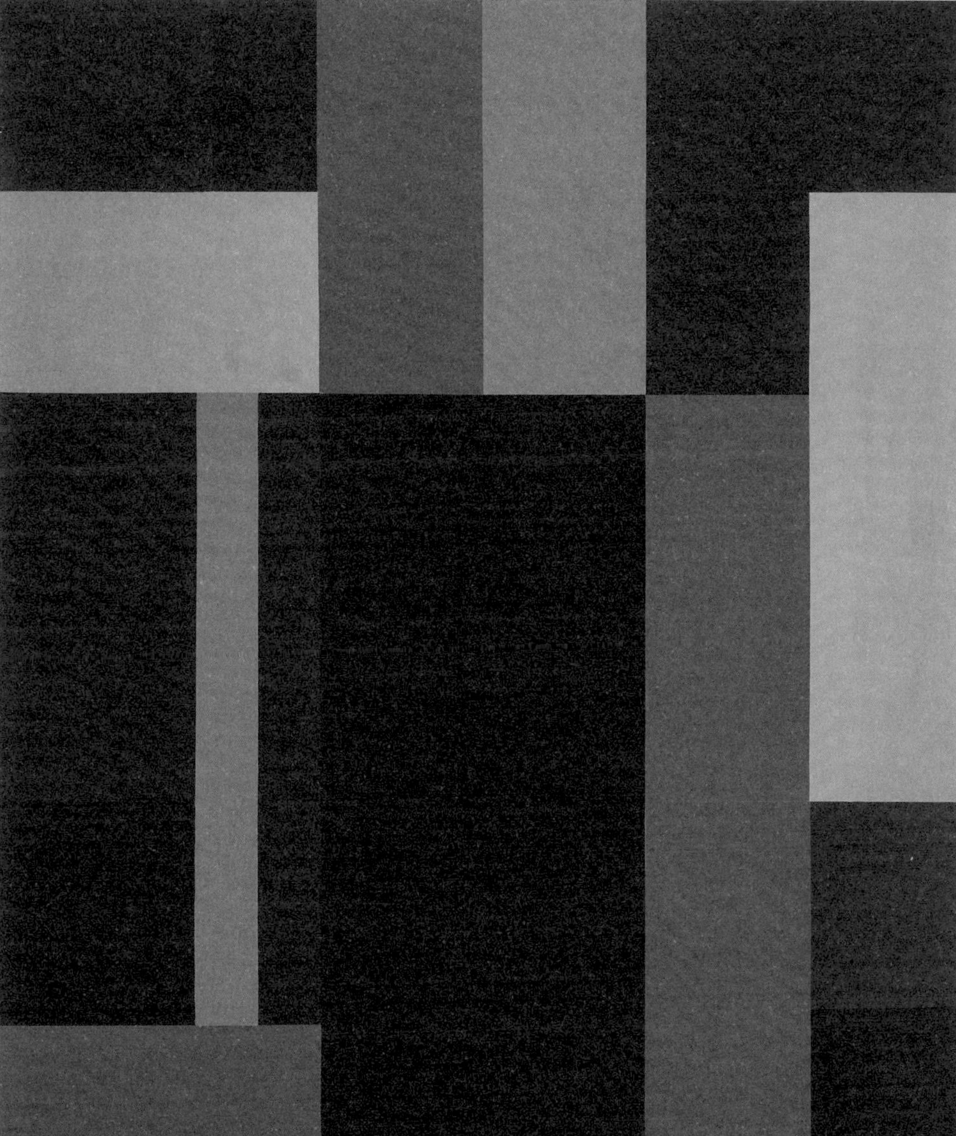

زياد كعكي

(مواليد 1993،
المملكة العربية السعودية)
يقيم ويعمل في جدة
(المملكة العربية السعودية)

زياد كعكي رسامٌ معروف باستخدامه الألوان الحيوية النابضة متأثراً بالتصوير الحراري والخلفيات التجريدية، حصل على درجة البكالوريوس في الفن والتصميم مع ريادة الأعمال من جامعة نورث إيسترن في بوسطن، الولايات المتحدة الأمريكية (2017)، وماجستير في الفنون الجميلة في الرسم من سنترال سانت مارتينز، في لندن، المملكة المتحدة (2021)، وتتميز أعماله بتركيزها على الهيئات البشرية، وبخاصة الأنثوية، واستكشافها لتأثير التكنولوجيا استناداً إلى تأثيرات عدسات الكاميرا والسمات الحيوانية لدى البشر.

عرض أعماله محلياً وعالمياً، ومن أبرز المعارض الجماعية التي شارك فيها "تعبيرات سينمائية" في غاليري ماريان إبراهيم بباريس، فرنسا (2022)؛ "نكست ويف" في معهد مسك للفنون بالرياض، المملكة العربية السعودية ومعهد برلين للفنون، ألمانيا (2022)؛ "HIRÆTH"، معرض "استكشاف" على الانترنت بتنظيم فيليبس في القنصلية الألمانية بجدة، المملكة العربية السعودية (2022)؛ "سبيستونز" بتنظيم معهد مسك للفنون في غاليري أثر بجدة، المملكة العربية السعودية (2021)؛ "بعيداً عن الكلمات" في مؤسسة كانديد للفنون، معرض خريجي سنترال سانت مارتينز بلندن، المملكة المتحدة (2021)؛ "صيرورات" في غاليري A.P.T. بلندن، المملكة المتحدة (2020)؛ "أعدك أن..." في استوديوات Apiary، معرض سنترال سانت مارتينز المؤقت بلندن، المملكة المتحدة (2020)؛ "من أجل حب الفن" في أحلام غاليري بالرياض، المملكة العربية السعودية (2019)؛ "دالتون واحد" في غاليري كانفاس للفنون التشكيلية ببوسطن، الولايات المتحدة الأمريكية (2018).

ZIAD KAKI

(b. 1993, Saudi Arabia)
Lives and works in Jeddah,
Saudi Arabia

Ziad Kaki is a painter known for his vibrant use of color, which was influenced by thermal imaging and abstracted backgrounds. He holds a bachelor's degree in art and design with entrepreneurship from Northeastern University, Boston, USA (2017) and an MFA in painting from Central Saint Martins, London, UK (2021). Often featuring human figures, particularly the female form, his art explores the impact of technology, drawing inspiration from camera-lens effects and the animalistic qualities within humans.

The artist has exhibited both locally and globally. Select group exhibitions include *Cinematic Expressions*, Mariane Ibrahim Gallery, Paris, France (2022); *Next Wave*, Misk Art Institute, Riyadh, Saudi Arabia, and Berlin Art Institute, Germany (2022); *HIRÆTH*, Phillips Online ISTIKSHAF Exhibition at the German Consulate, Jeddah, Saudi Arabia (2022); *Spacetoons*, organized by Misk Art Institute, ATHR Gallery, Jeddah, Saudi Arabia (2021); *Away with Words*, Candid Arts Trust, Central St Martins Graduate Show, London, UK (2021); Becomings, A.P.T. Gallery, London, UK (2020); *I Promise You...*, Apiary Studios, Central St Martins Interim Show, London, UK (2020); *For the Love of Art*, Ahlam Gallery, Riyadh, Saudi Arabia (2019); and *One Dalton*, Canvas Fine Arts, Boston, USA (2018).

زيــاد ككــي

(مواليد 1993، المملكة العربية السعودية)

مراقبة، 2019

زيت على قماش
41 × 51 سم
بإذن من الفنان

ZIAD KAKI

(b. 1993, Saudi Arabia)

Surveillance, 2019

Oil on canvas
41 × 51 cm
Courtesy of the artist

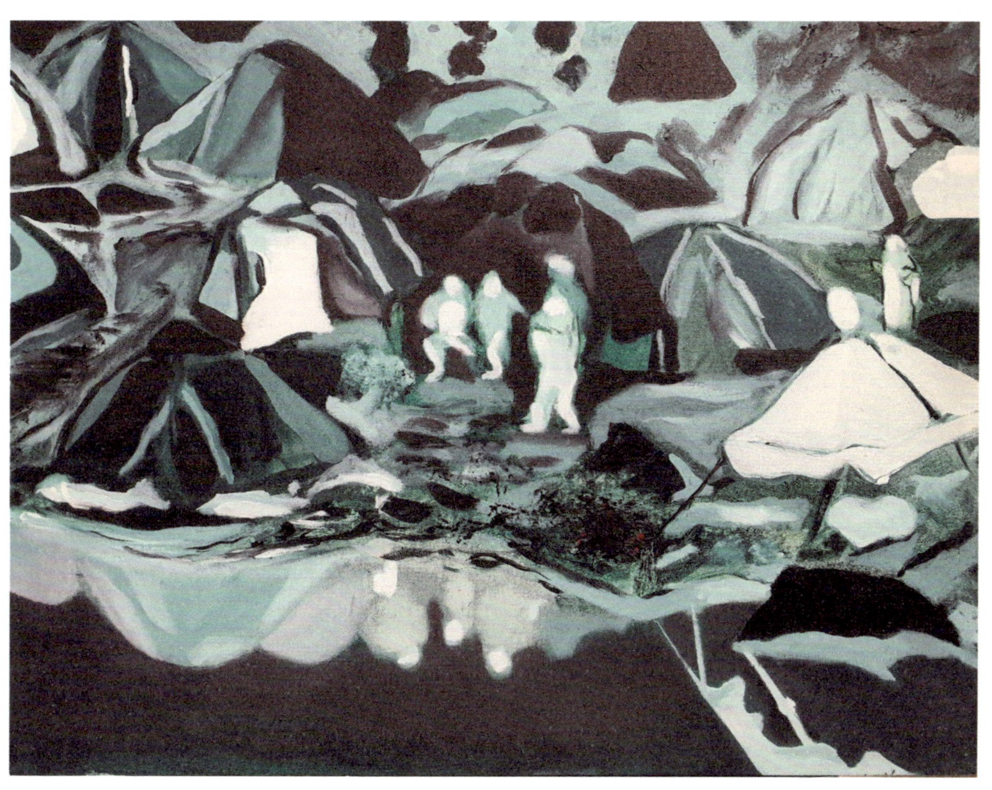

خالـــد مخشـــوش

(مواليد 1992،
المملكة العربية السعودية)
يقيم ويعمل في الرياض
(المملكة العربية السعودية)

خالـد مخشـوش فنـانٌ رقمـي متخصـص في فن عناصر الصـورة (البيكسـل)، أمضى عاماً في دراسـة علم الفلك في جامعة شمال أريزونا، قبل أن يتوجّه إلى مهنة الفن، وبـدأ بالتعبير البصـري المتجذر في المجـال الرقمـي فـي عـام 2016 مدفوعاً بشغفه باللعـب وتطويـر ألعـاب الفيديـو، وهـو لا يـزال يسـتلهم مـن الرسـومات الرقميـة المبكـرة وأجهزة الألعـاب، ويسـتخدم فـي لوحاتـه الرقميـة ألـواح الرسـم والأقلام والفأرة الرقمية، ويصور فيها مناظر للمواقـع الحضريـة والريفيـة والتاريخيـة، بمـا فـي ذلـك الطرق السـريعة والمواقـع الصناعية والمدن، ينظـر إلى فـن عناصـر الصـورة (البيكسـل) على أنه وسـيط مضغـوط ولكنـه يتمتـع بقوة تعبيرية إبداعيـة من حيـث الإمكانيـات التي تتيحهـا الألوان والأشكال والأنماط لاستكشاف المساحات الوجدانية والجسدية والافتراضية، والتوصل إلى مَشاهد تدمج بين الابتـكار الرقمـي والثقافـة التقليديـة.

شـارك مخشـوش فـي العديـد مـن المعارض الجماعيـة، مـن أبرزهـا "مسـاحة 036" في غاليري أسـبراي اسـتوديو ومؤسسـة سـيغ للفنـون بلنـدن، المملكـة المتحـدة (2023)؛ و"نـور الريـاض" فـي الريـاض، المملكـة العربيـة السـعودية (2023)؛ وحفـل افتتـاح فعاليـة "نـور الريـاض" فـي غاليـري أوترنت بلنـدن، المملكة المتحـدة (2023)؛ و"حافة الجزيـرة العربية العربية X يلا سـواب" في الرياض، المملكة العربية السعودية (2022)، وفي عام 2023، شارك في برنامـج الإقامة الفنيـة في اليونان الـذي تدعمه وزارة الثقافة في المملكة العربية السعودية وتديره مؤسسـة سـيغ للفنون.

KHALED MAKHSHOUSH

(b. 1992, Saudi Arabia)
Lives and works in Riyadh,
Saudi Arabia

Khaled Makhshoush is a self-taught digital artist specializing in pixel art. After graduating from high school, he spent a year studying astronomy at Northern Arizona University, after which he left the program to pursue a career in art. Rooted in the digital realm, his visual expression began in 2016, ignited by his passion for playing and developing video games. He still often draws inspiration from early computer graphics and game consoles. The artist uses a drawing tablet, stylus, and mouse in his digital paintings, which often portray detailed scenes from urban, rural, and historical locations, including highways, industrial sites, and cities. He perceives pixel art as a compact yet potent medium for creative expression, employing colors, shapes, and patterns to explore emotional, physical, and virtual spaces while weaving scenes that fuse digital innovation with traditional culture.

Makhshoush has participated in numerous group exhibitions, including *Surface 036*, Asprey Studio Gallery x Sigg Art Foundation, London, UK (2023); Noor Riyadh, Riyadh, Saudi Arabia (2023); the Noor Riyadh Launch Event, Outernet, London, UK (2023); and Edge of Arabia x Yallaswap, Riyadh, Saudi Arabia (2022). In 2023, he took part in The Greek Residency program, supported by the Ministry of Culture, Saudi Arabia and operated by the Sigg Art Foundation.

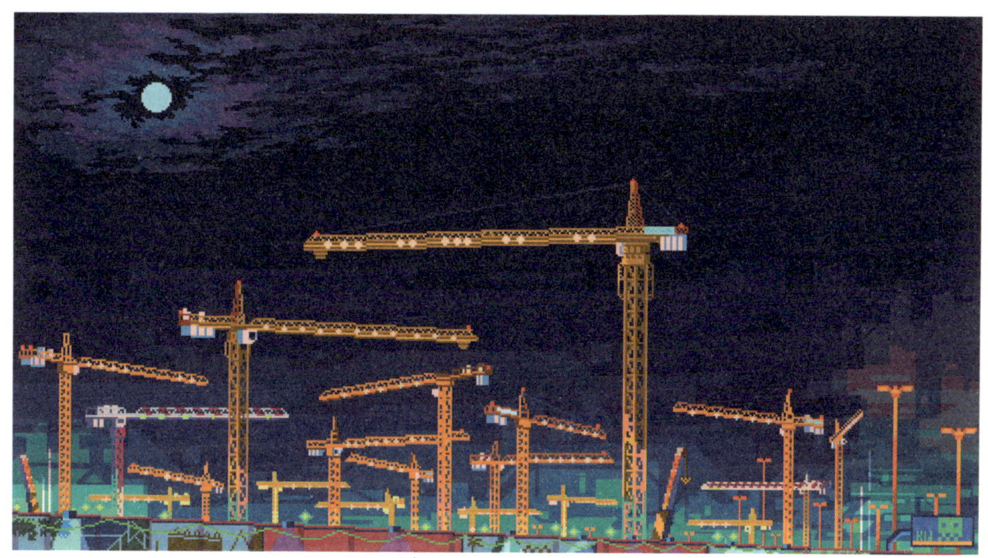

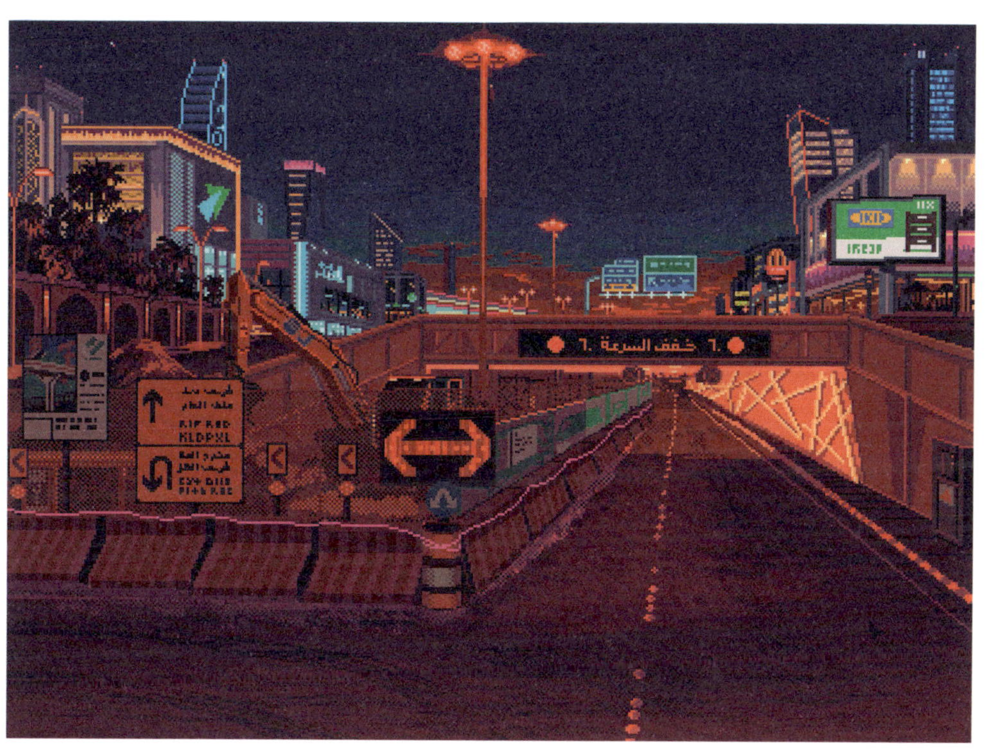
٦٠ خفف السرعة ٦٠
طريق دبي
مطار الطائف
RIF RBD
KLDPXL
مشروع الطائف
طريق القطر
E34 D110
PI+6 R32

أحمد ماطر

(مواليد 1979،
المملكة العربية السعودية)
يقيم ويعمل في الرياض
(المملكة العربية السعودية)

أحمد ماطر فنانٌ مفاهيمي متعدد الوسائط، يعمل على توثيق الواقع المعاصر في المملكة العربية السعودية، وضع أولى خطواته في عالم الفن رسمياً في عام 1999 عندما انضم إلى قرية المفتاحة التشكيلية التي يحتضنها مركز الملك فهد الثقافي، تحت رعاية صاحب السمو الملكي الأمير خالد الفيصل، وكان له محترَفه الخاص، وقد تلقّى المعارف الفنية على يد فنانين سعوديين رائدين مثل عبد الحليم رضوي في منتصف العقد الأول من القرن الحادي والعشرين. تخرّج أحمد ماطر من كلية الطب في جامعة الملك خالد بأبها، وشارك في تأسيس مبادرة "حافة الجزيرة العربية" للفن المعاصر في عام 2008؛ يستكشف في أعماله الفنية الذكريات الجماعية لكشف وتسجيل التاريخ غير الرسمي من خلال الأفلام والفيديو والتصوير الفوتوغرافي والتركيبات الفنية والنحت والأداء، ويستخدم مجموعة من تقنيات التقصي من أجل إعادة تشكيل التاريخ والوقائع الاجتماعية والسياسية غير الرسمية من منظار عدسة المراقب، ما يسمح له بوضع تقييم لحالة المملكة وصياغة التكهنات عن مستقبل هذا البلد الذي يتمتع بنفوذ ديني واجتماعي واقتصادي وسياسي لا مثيل له.

عُرضت أعمال أحمد ماطر محلياً ودولياً؛ فقد شارك في العديد من المعارض الجماعية، من أبرزها بينالي أورليان للعمارة بفرنسا (2019-2020)؛ وشارك في أعمال كـ"الحنين إلى مكة" في متحف تروبين بأمستردام، هولندا (2019)؛ و"من خلال الطيف" في غاليري أثر بجدة، المملكة العربية السعودية (2018)؛ و"الحج في رحاب الرحلة" في متحف الفن الإسلامي بالدوحة، قطر (2013)؛ و"نهوض - نحو خريطة ثقافية جديدة"، في بينالي الشارقة بالإمارات العربية المتحدة (2013)؛ و"أشغال داخلية 6"، في مقر الجمعية اللبنانية للفنون التشكيلية (أشكال ألوان) ببيروت، لبنان (2013)؛ و"25 عاماً من الإبداع العربي" في معهد العالم العربي بباريس، فرنسا (2013)؛ وبينالي كوتشي-موزيريس في كيرالا بالهند (2012)؛ وبينالي البندقية، بإيطاليا (2009)؛ وبينالي القاهرة بمصر (2008)؛ و"كلمة في الفن: فنانو الشرق الأوسط الحديث" في المتحف البريطاني بلندن، المملكة المتحدة (2006). كما أقام العديد من المعارض الفردية، من بينها "أحمد ماطر: تذروه الرياح"، كريستيز بلندن، المملكة المتحدة (2024)؛ "أحمد ماطر: رحلات مكة" في متحف بروكلين بنيويورك، الولايات المتحدة الأمريكية (2019)؛ و"بين كيف وكيف" في مدينة الملك عبدالله الاقتصادية، المملكة العربية السعودية (2018)؛ "ميتوكوندريا: مركز الطاقة" في غاليري كونتينوا بسان جيمينيانو، إيطاليا (2017)؛ و"مدن رمزية" في غاليري آرثر ساكلر بمؤسسة سميثسونيان في واشنطن العاصمة، الولايات المتحدة الأمريكية (2016)؛ و"العثور على 100 قطعة" في مؤسسة الشارقة للفنون، الإمارات العربية المتحدة (2013)؛ و"أحمد ماطر في فينيل فاكتوري" في غاليري فينيل فاكتوري بلندن، المملكة المتحدة (2010).

دخلت أعماله إلى كبريات المجموعات الفنية، كمجموعة المتحف البريطاني بلندن، المملكة المتحدة؛ ومتحف فيكتوريا وألبرت بلندن، المملكة المتحدة؛ ومتحف مقاطعة لوس أنجلوس للفنون، الولايات المتحدة الأمريكية؛ ومتحف الفن الإسلامي بالدوحة، قطر؛ ومركز بومبيدو بباريس، فرنسا.

AHMED MATER

(b. 1979, Saudi Arabia)
Lives and works in Riyadh,
Saudi Arabia

Ahmed Mater is a multimedia conceptual artist who documents the realities of contemporary Saudi Arabia. He formally entered the art world in 1999, when he joined Al-Meftaha Arts Village, part of the King Fahd Cultural Centre, under the patronage of HRH Prince Khalid Alfaisal. There, he had his own studio and studied under pioneering Saudi artists such as Abdulhalim Radwi. In the mid-aughts, he trained as a physician at King Khalid University, Abha College of Medicine, and in 2008, he cofounded the contemporary art initiative Edge of Arabia. His practice explores collective memories to uncover and record unofficial histories through film, video, photography, immersive installation, sculpture, and performance. Mater employs broad investigative techniques to reframe unofficial sociopolitical histories and realities with an observational and wide-ranging scope, thus assessing Saudi Arabia's condition. Through this lens, he imagines possible prognoses for a land of unprecedented religious, social, economic, and political influence.

Mater's work has been widely exhibited locally and internationally. He has participated in group exhibitions including Biennale d'Architecture d'Orléans, France (2019–20); *Longing for Mecca*, Tropenmuseum, Amsterdam, The Netherlands (2019); *Through the Spectrum*, Athr Gallery, Jeddah, Saudi Arabia (2018); *Hajj: The Journey through Art*, Museum of Islamic Art, Doha, Qatar (2013); *Re:Emerge Towards a New Cultural Cartography*, Sharjah Biennial, UAE (2013); *Home Works 6*, Ashkal Alwan, Beirut, Lebanon (2013); *25 Years of Arab Creativity*, Institut du monde arabe, Paris, France (2013); the Kochi-Muziris Biennale, Kerala, India (2012); the 53rd Venice Biennale, Italy (2009); the Cairo Biennale, Egypt (2008); and *Word into Art: Artists of the Modern Middle East*, British Museum, London, UK (2006), among others. He has also held numerous solo exhibitions, including *Ahmed Mater: Chronicles*, Christie's, London, UK (2024); *Ahmed Mater: Mecca Journeys*, Brooklyn Museum, New York, USA (2019); *Drum Roll, Please*, King Abdullah Economic City, Saudi Arabia (2018); *Mitochondria: Powerhouses*, Galleria Continua, San Gimignano, Italy (2017); *Symbolic Cities*, Arthur M. Sackler Gallery, Smithsonian Institution, Washington, D.C., USA (2016); *100 Found Objects*, Sharjah Art Foundation, UAE (2013); and *Ahmed Mater at Vinyl Factory*, Vinyl Factory, London, UK (2010).

His work is part of major collections, including those of the British Museum, London, UK; the Victoria & Albert Museum, London, UK; the Los Angeles County Museum of Art, USA; the Museum of Islamic Art, Doha, Qatar; and the Centre Pompidou, Paris, France.

أحمـــد ماطـــر
(مواليد 1979، المملكة العربية السعودية)

الهوائي الأخضر، 2010

أنبوب نيون
150 × 150 × 50 سم
بإذن من الفنان ومجموعة بسمة السليمان
لذكرى محمد الجفالي

AHMED MATER
(b. 1979, Saudi Arabia)

Green Antenna, 2010

Neon tube
150 × 150 × 50 cm
Courtesy of the artist and Basma Alsulaiman Collection
In loving memory of Mohammed Aljuffali

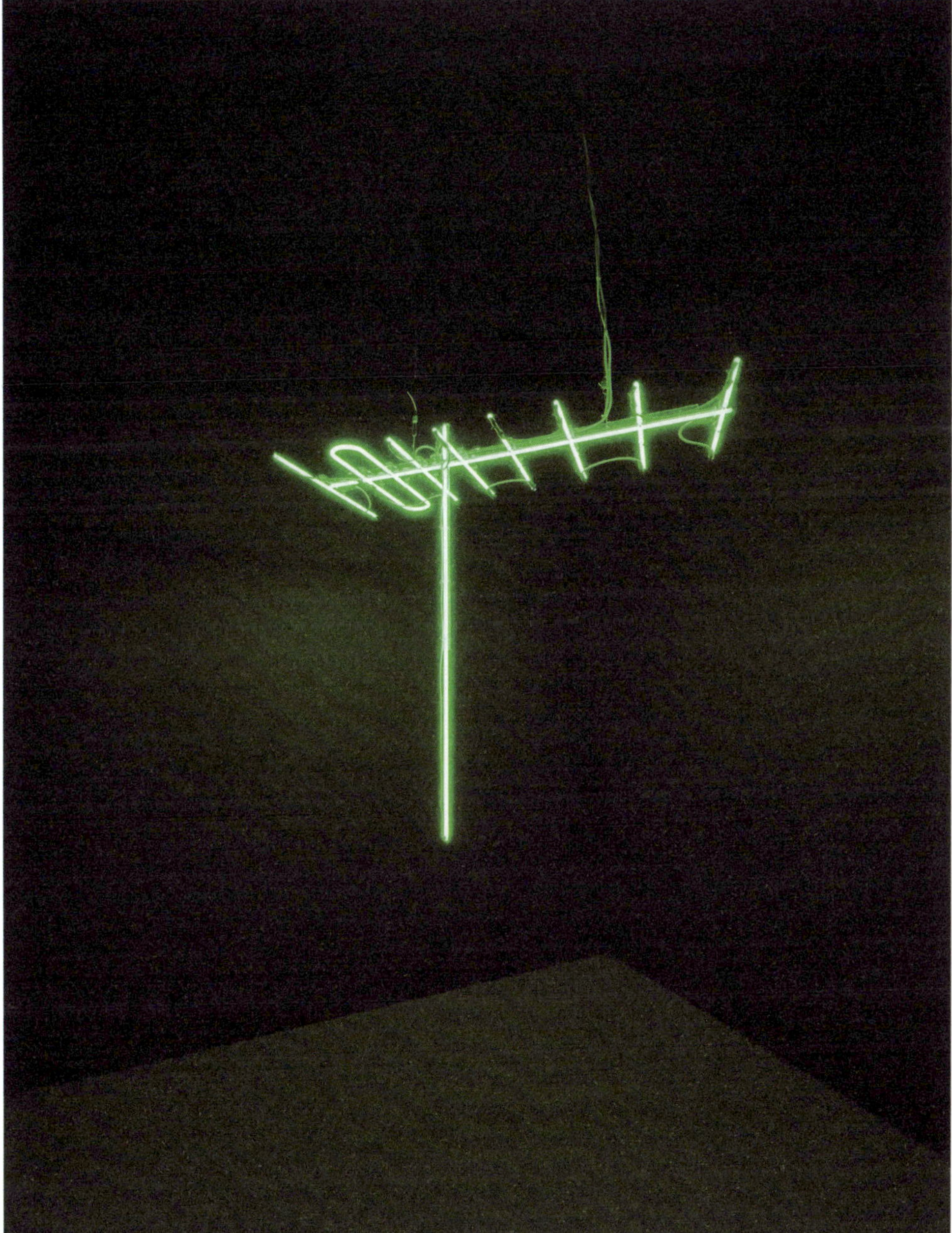

بينيت ميلر

(مواليد 1966،
الولايات المتحدة الأمريكية)
يقيم ويعمل في نيويورك
(الولايات المتحدة الأمريكية)

كان بينيت ميلر في الأساس صانع أفلام ومخرج سينمائي، وقد خاض مؤخراً في مجال الفنون البصرية مستكشفاً إمكانات الذكاء الاصطناعي من خلال أعمال موَلّدة خوارزمياً، وهو ينظر في مزاولته الفنية في التحولات التي تؤدي إليها التكنولوجيا في كيفية إدراك الواقع؛ وُلد لأم رسامة وأب مهندس، ودرس في مدرسة تيش للفنون بجامعة نيويورك، لكنه ترك الدراسة قبل وقت قصير من تخرجه، وبدأ حياته المهنية في مجال السينما بإخراج الفيلم الوثائقي "الرحلة البحرية" (ذا كروز) عام 1998، وهو فيلم بالأبيض والأسود يدور حول شخصية تيموثي سبيد ليفيتش الدليل السياحي في نيويورك.

أقيم أول معرضين فرديين لميلر في الولايات المتحدة، في غاليريات غاغوسيان في بيفرلي هيلز (2024) ونيويورك (2023) كما أخرج ثلاثة أفلام روائية طويلة، وهي "كابوتي" (2005)، و"كرة المال" (موني بول) (2011) و"صائد الثعالب" (فوكس كاتشر) (2014).

فاز بالعديد من الجوائز في مسيرته السينمائية، من بينها جائزة الروح المستقلة للتميّز الخاص (2014) وجائزة أفضل مخرج في مهرجان كان السينمائي (2014) كما ترشّح لجوائز متعددة، بما فيها جائزة السعفة الذهبية في مهرجان كان السينمائي (2014)؛ وجائزة الأوسكار لأفضل مخرج (2005 و2014)؛ وجائزة الأكاديمية البريطانية لأفضل مخرج (2005)؛ وجائزة نقابة المخرجين الأمريكيين لأفضل مخرج (2005)؛ وجائزة نقابة المنتجين الأمريكيين للإنتاج المتميز (2014).

BENNETT MILLER

(b. 1966, USA)
Lives and works in New York, USA

Bennett Miller is primarily a filmmaker and director who has recently ventured into visual art, exploring the potential of artificial intelligence with algorithmically generated works. Within his art practice, he examines the tech-driven shift in perception of reality and truth. Born to a painter mother and an engineer father, he attended New York University's Tisch School of the Arts, but he dropped out shortly before graduating. He began his film career by directing the 1998 documentary, *The Cruise*, a black-and-white film that centers on Timothy "Speed" Levitch, a New York City tour guide.

Miller's first two solo exhibitions were held in the USA, at Gagosian, Beverly Hills (2024), and Gagosian, New York (2023). He also directed the feature films *Capote* (2005), *Moneyball* (2011), and *Foxcatcher* (2014).

He has won several awards related to his film career, including the Special Distinction Award at the Independent Spirit Awards (2014) and Best Director at the Cannes Film Festival (2014). He was also nominated for multiple awards, including the Palme d'Or at the Cannes Film Festival (2014); Best Director at the Academy Awards (2005 and 2014); Best Director at the British Academy Film Awards (2005); Best Director at the Directors Guild of America Awards (2005); and Outstanding Producer at the Producers Guild of America Awards (2014).

(مواليد 1966، الولايات المتحدة الأمريكية)

بدون عنوان، 2022-2023

طباعة صبغية لصورة مولدة بواسـطة الذكاء الاصطناعي
85.7 × 85.7 سم
بإذن من الفنان وغاليري غاغوسيان

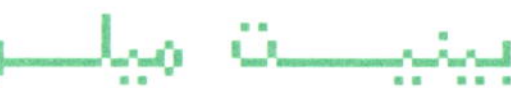

BENNETT MILLER
(b. 1966, USA)

Untitled, 2022–2023

Pigment print of an AI-generated image
85.7 × 85.7 cm
Courtesy of the artist and Gagosian

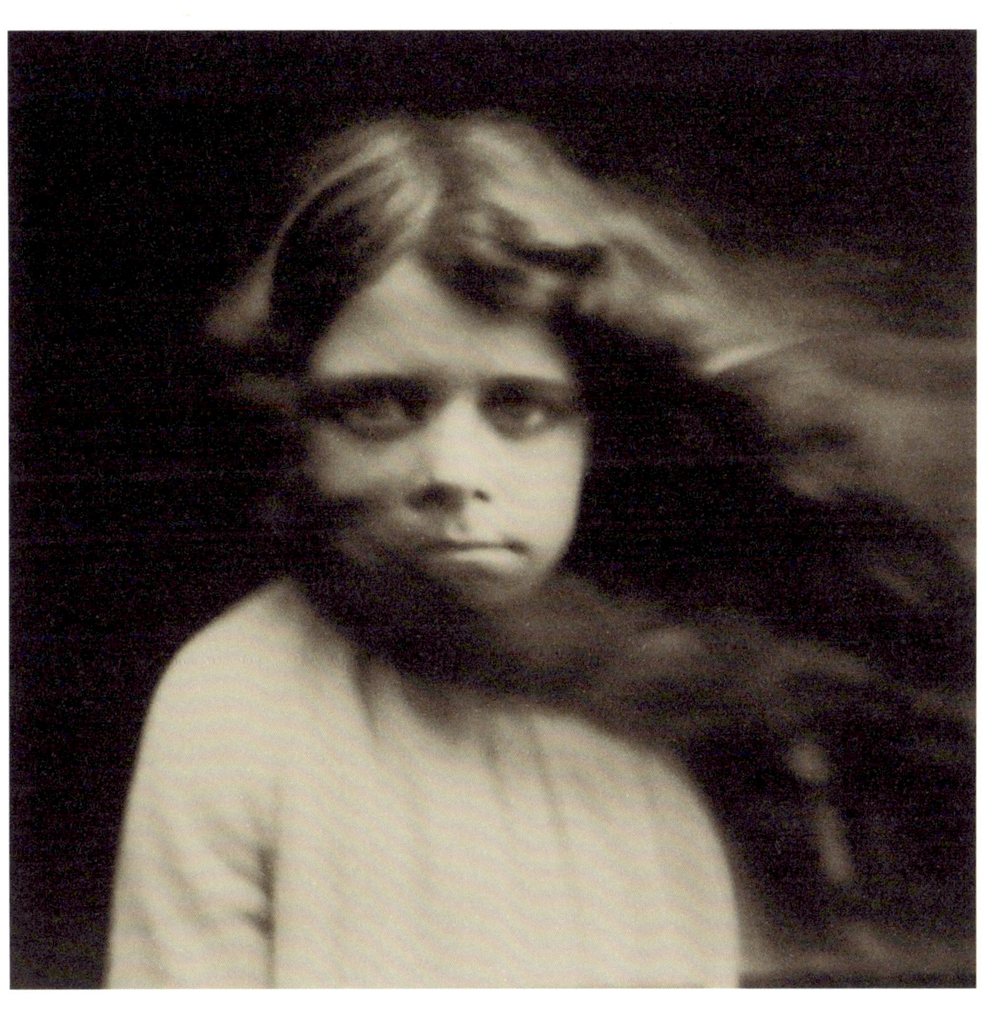

(مواليد 1966، الولايات المتحدة الأمريكية)

بدون عنوان، 2022-2023

طباعة صبغية لصورة مولدة بواسـطة الذكاء الاصطناعي
85.7 × 85.7 سم
بإذن من الفنان وغاليري غاغوسيان

BENNETT MILLER

(b. 1966, USA)

Untitled, 2022–2023

Pigment print of an AI-generated image
85.7 × 85.7 cm
Courtesy of the artist and Gagosian

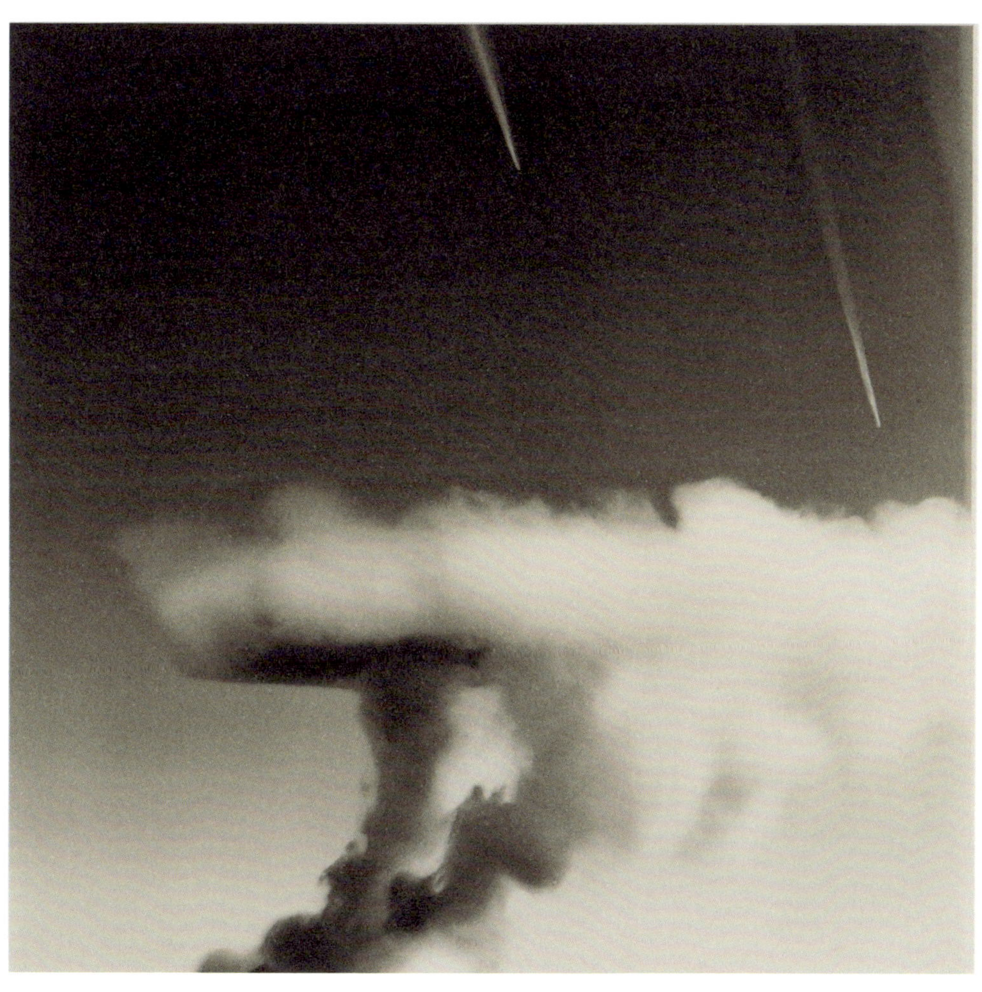

BENNETT MILLER

(b. 1966, USA)

Untitled, 2022–2023

Pigment print of an AI-generated image
85.7 × 85.7 cm
Courtesy of the artist and Gagosian

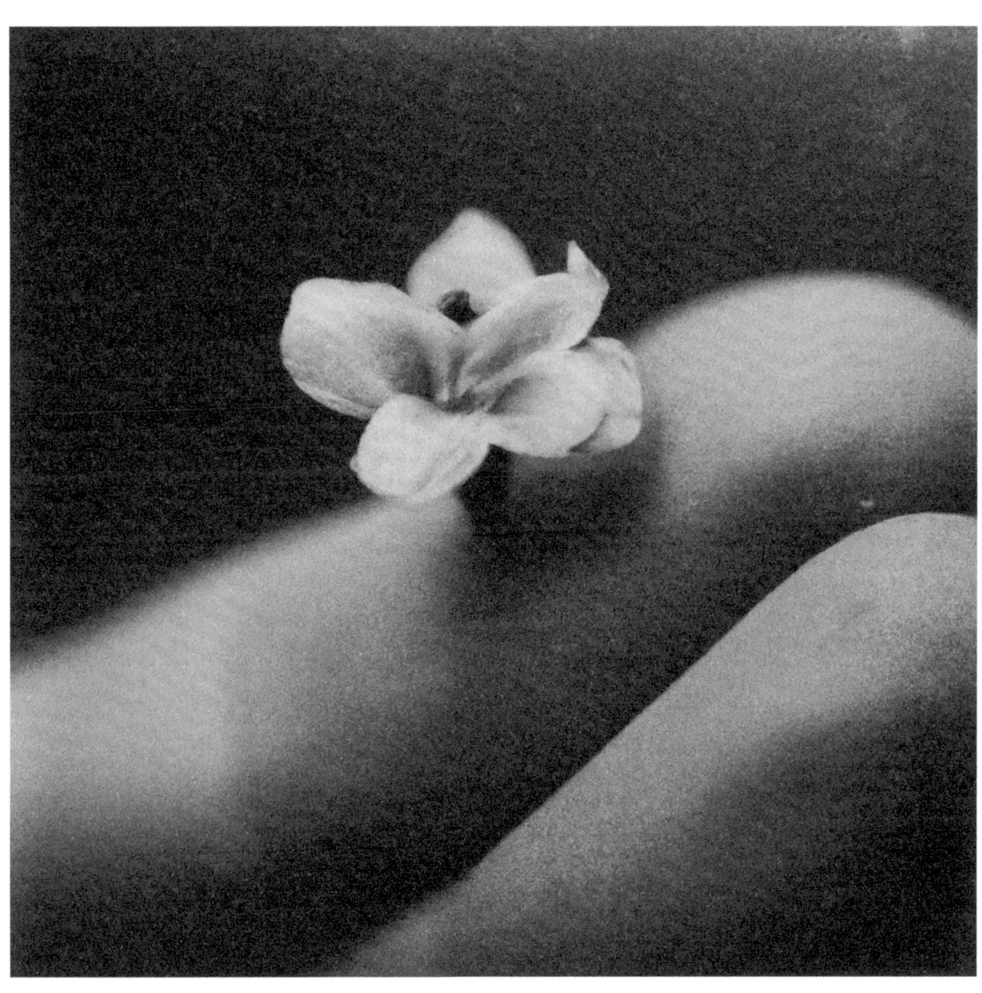

نـــام جـــون بايـــك

(مواليد 1932، كوريا الجنوبية – وتوفي 2006، الولايات المتحدة الأمريكية)

كان نام جـون بايك فناناً متعدد الوسائط معروفاً بعملـه في فـن الفيديو، وُلـد فـي كوريـا الجنوبية، وتعـرّف علـى الموسيقى فـي سـن مبكـرة، وخاصة مـن خـلال دروس البيانـو والتأليـف، والتـي وضعت الأسـاس لرحلتـه الفنية، فـي عـام 1956، تخرج من جامعة طوكيو بشـهادة في علم الجمـال، ثم انتقل إلى ألمانيـا حيـث واصـل دراسـة تاريـخ الموسـيقى فـي جامعة ميونيـخ والتقى بعـدد مـن الملحنين الطليعيـيـن، مثـل جون كيـج، الذين أثروا فـي رؤيـته الفنية. درس التأليف الموسيقي في معهد فرايبورغ للموسـيقى فـي ألمانيا. وفـي عـام 1964، انتقل إلى الولايات المتحدة فـي منعطف حاسـم وانكـب علـى التجريـب فـي فـن الفيديـو، ما وضع الأسـاس لمسـاهماته فـي هـذا الميدان. ومـع تطـور مزاولته الفنية، جمـع بين فـن الفيديو والنحـت والتركيب، وكان رائداً فـي الأداء والفن المبني على التكنولوجيا، حيـث حقق إنجازات مهمة فـي السـتينيات من القرن العشـرين، بما فـي ذلـك أنه أصبـح أول فنان يعرض الأشـكال التجريدية على الشاشات ويسـتخدم كاميرا الفيديـو الصغيـرة المحمولة فـي عمله.

شـارك بايـك فـي أكثر من مائة معرض جماعي على مستوى العالم، من أبرزها؛ "القرن الأمريكي: فن وثقافة، 1900-2000 (الجزء الثاني)" وفي متحف ويتنـي للفن الأمريكي بنيويورك، الولايـات المتحدة الأمريكيـة (1999)؛ و"فـي أرجاء إسطنبول"، بينالي إسطنبول الدولـي الرابـع، تركيا (1995)؛ متحـف بينالي كوانجو للفن المعاصر، كوانجو، كوريا الجنوبية (1995)؛ و"الفن الياباني بعد عام 1945: صرخة في وجه السـماء" فـي متحف يوكوهاما للفنون، اليابان (1994)؛ و"السـفر إلـى نيويورك" فـي غوغنهايم سـوهو، نيويـورك، الولايـات المتحدة الأمريكية

(1995)؛ بينالـي سـيدني الثامن، أسـتراليا (1990)؛ و"فنون التلفزيون" في متحف الفن المعاصر بلوس أنجلوس، الولايات المتحدة الأمريكية (1987)؛ بينالي البندقية الحادي والأربعون (1984)؛ و"فن الفيديو في الولايات المتحدة الأمريكية"، بينالي سـاو باولـو الثالـث عشـر، البرازيل (1975)، كما أقام أكثر من سـتين معرضاً فرديـاً، من بينها "نام جون بايك" في غاليري أسـبايك بكوبنهاغـن، الدنمارك (1996)؛ و"نـام جون بايك: نحـت الفيديو" فـي غاليري مايور بلندن، المملكة المتحدة (1991)؛ و"نام جون بايك" في مركز بومبيدو - المتحف الوطني للفن الحديث بباريـس، فرنسـا (1982)؛ و"سلسـلة صنّاع الأفلام الأمريكيين الجدد، نام جون بايك" في متحف ويتني للفن الأمريكي بنيويورك، الولايات المتحدة الأمريكية (1980)؛ و"معرض نام جون بايك الاسـتعادي" في متحف بلدية باريس للفن الحديث، فرنسا (1979).

دخـلت أعماله إلى أكثر من خمسـين مجموعة فنيـة عامة، من بينها مجموعـة متحـف غوغنهايم نيويـورك، الولايـات المتحـدة الأمريكـية؛ ومتحـف هيروشيما، اليابان؛ ومتحف لونغ بشنغهاي، الصين؛ ومتحـف مقاطعة لوس أنجلوس للفنون، الولايات المتحـدة الأمريكيـة؛ ومتحف الفن المعاصـر فـي مؤسسة إيدلمان بلوزان، سويسرا؛ والمتحف الوطني للفن الحديث بباريـس، فرنسـا؛ ومركـز بومبيدو بباريـس، فرنسـا؛ ومتحـف الفـن المعاصـر بطوكيو، اليابـان؛ ومتحف الفن الحديـث بنيويورك، الولايات المتحـدة الأمريكيـة؛ ومتحـف سميثسـونيان للفن الأمريكـي بواشـنطن العاصمـة، الولايات المتحـدة الأمريكـي؛ وتيت مـودرن بلندن، المملكـة المتحدة؛ ومتحف ويتني للفن الأمريكي بنيويورك، الولايات الأمريكيـة. وعلى مر السـنين، حصل بايك علـى العديد من الجوائز المختلفة، من بينها جائزة الأسد الذهبي لبينالي البندقية عام 1993.

NAM JUNE PAIK

Nam June Paik was a multimedia artist known for his pioneering work in video art. Born in South Korea, he was exposed to music at an early age, particularly through piano and composition lessons, which laid the foundation for his artistic journey. In 1956, Paik graduated from the University of Tokyo with a degree in aesthetics. He then moved to Germany, where he continued to study the history of music at the University of Munich. There, he encountered avant-garde composers, such as John Cage, who shaped his artistic vision. Paik also studied composition at Freiburg Conservatory of Music in Germany. In 1964, the artist made a pivotal move to the USA, where he began to experiment with video art, laying the groundwork for his contributions to the field. As he developed his practice, he combined video art with sculpture and installation. Paik was as a pioneer in performance and technology-based art, making significant breakthroughs in the 1960s, including becoming the first artist to showcase abstract forms on screens and utilizing a small portable video camera within his work.

Paik participated in more than one hundred group exhibitions globally. Select presentations include *The American Century: Art and Culture, 1900–2000 (Part 2)*, Whitney Museum of American Art, New York, USA (1999); *Istanbul, throughout the City*, 4th International Istanbul Biennial, Turkey (1995); Kwangju Biennale Museum of Contemporary Art, Kwangju, South Korea (1995); *Japanese Art after 1945: Scream against the Sky*, Yokohama Museum of Art, Japan (1994), *Traveled to New York*, Guggenheim SoHo, New York, USA (1995); 8th Biennale of Sydney, Australia (1990); *The Arts for Television*, Museum of Contemporary Art, Los Angeles, USA (1987); 41st Venice Biennale, Italy (1984); and *Video Art USA*, XIII Bienal de São Paolo, Brazil (1975), among others. The artist also held more than sixty solo exhibitions, including *Nam June Paik*, Asbaek Gallery, Copenhagen, Denmark (1996); *Nam June Paik: Video Sculpture*, the Mayor Gallery, London, UK (1991); *Nam June Paik*, Centre Pompidou, Paris, France (1982); *The New American Filmmakers Series, Nam June Paik*, Whitney Museum of American Art, New York, USA (1980); and *Nam June Paik Rétrospective*, Musée d'Art Moderne de Paris, Ville de Paris, France (1979).

The artist's work is held in more than fifty public collections, including those of the Guggenheim New York, USA; the Hiroshima Museum, Japan; the Long Museum, Shanghai, China; the Los Angeles County Museum of Art, USA; the Musee d'Art Contemporain, Foundation Edelman, Lausanne, Switzerland; Musée National d'Art Moderne, Paris, France; Centre Pompidou, Paris, France; the Museum of Contemporary Art, Tokyo, Japan; the Museum of Modern Art, New York, USA; the Smithsonian American Art Museum, Washington, D.C., USA; the Tate Modern, London, UK; and the Whitney Museum of American Art, New York, USA. Over the years, Paik also was awarded various prizes, including the Golden Lion at the 45th Venice Biennale (1993).

NAM JUNE PAIK

(b. 1932, South Korea
d. 2006, USA)

Untitled, 2005

Single-channel video (color, silent), acrylic and permanent
oil marker on a monitor in a metal vintage television cabinet
60 × 35.6 × 41.9 cm
© Nam June Paik Estate

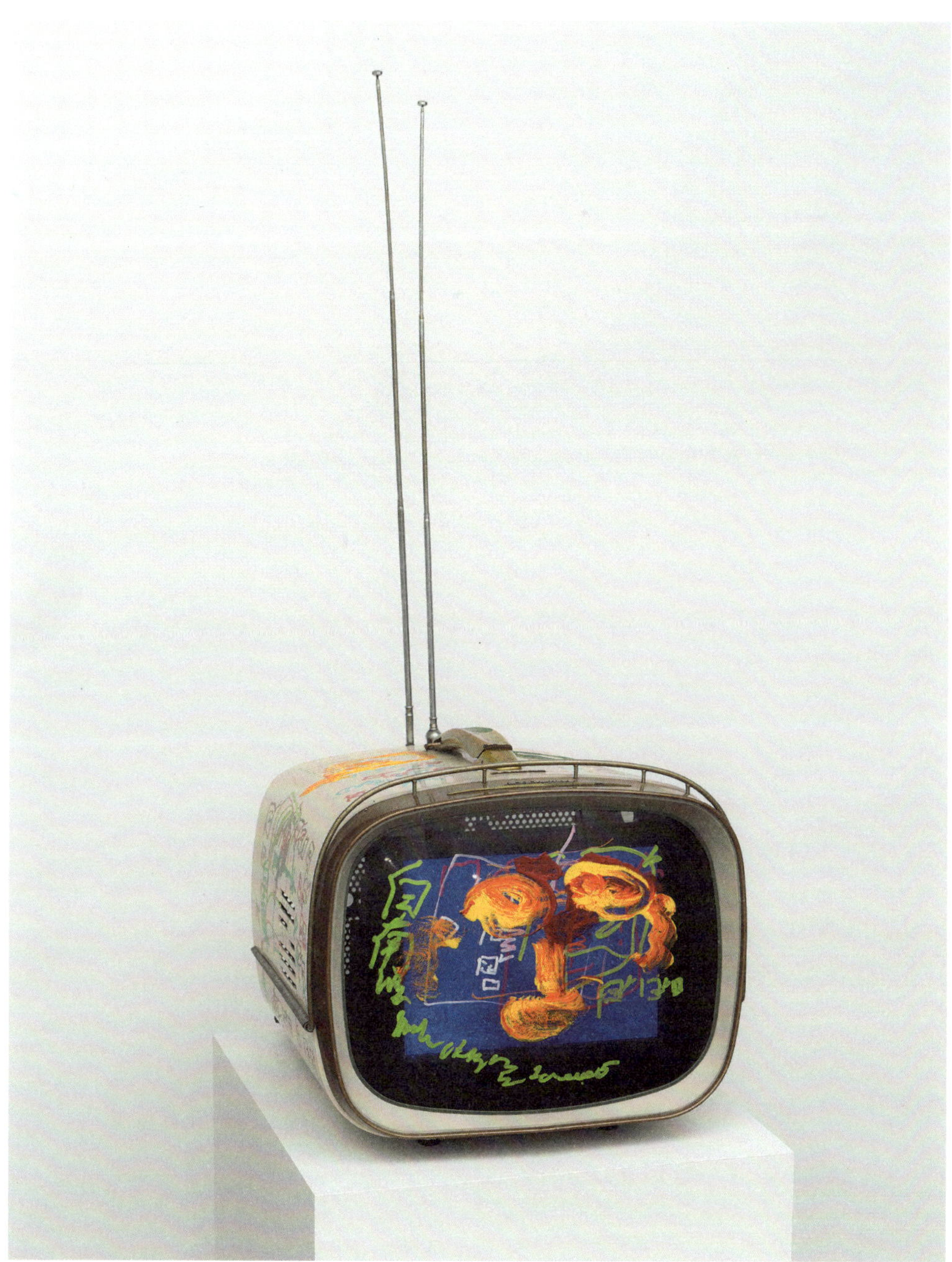

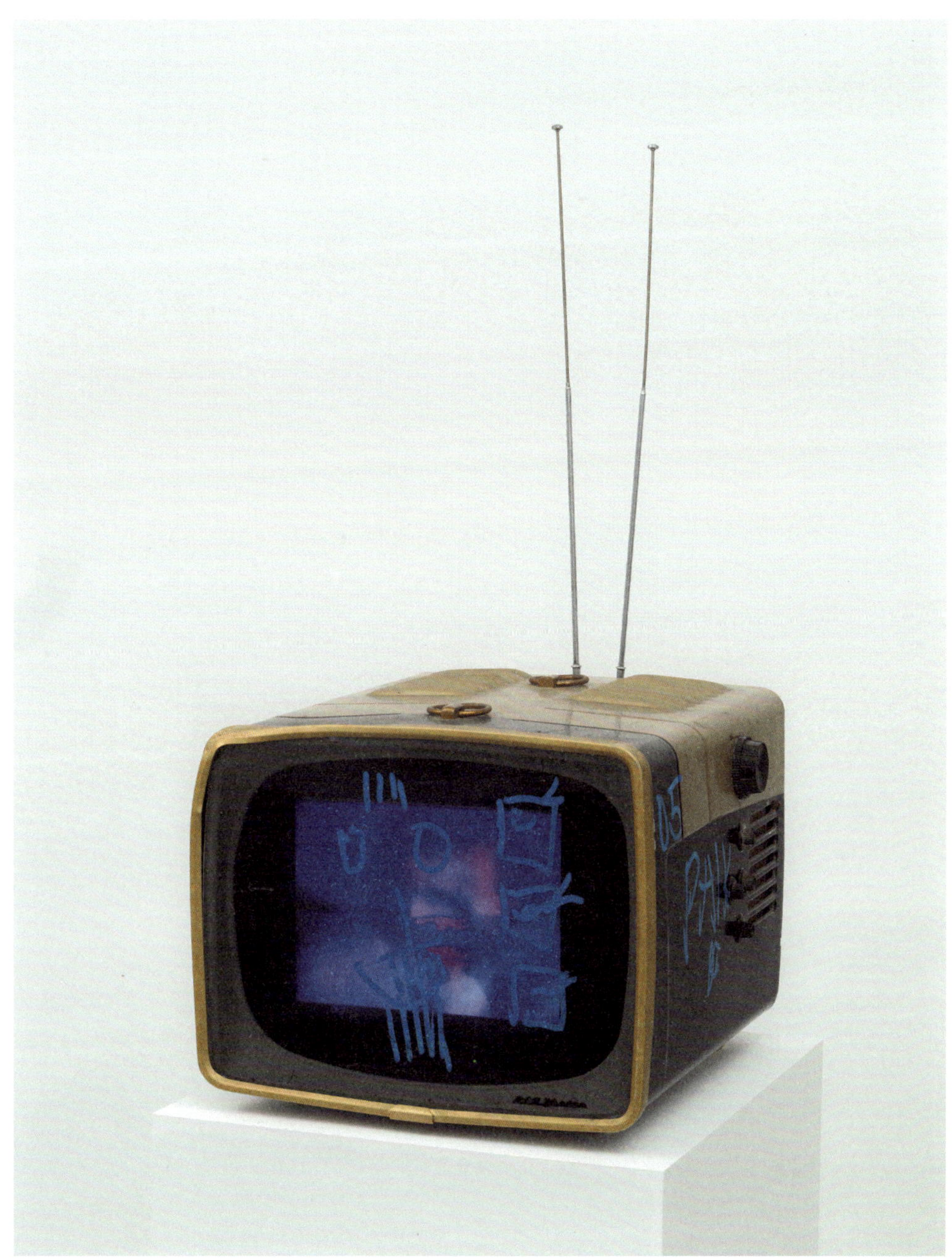

نام جـــون بايـــك

(1932، كوريا الجنوبية – 2006،
الولايات المتحدة الأمريكية)

بدون عنوان، 2005

NAM JUNE PAIK

(b. 1932, South Korea
d. 2006, USA)

Untitled, 2005

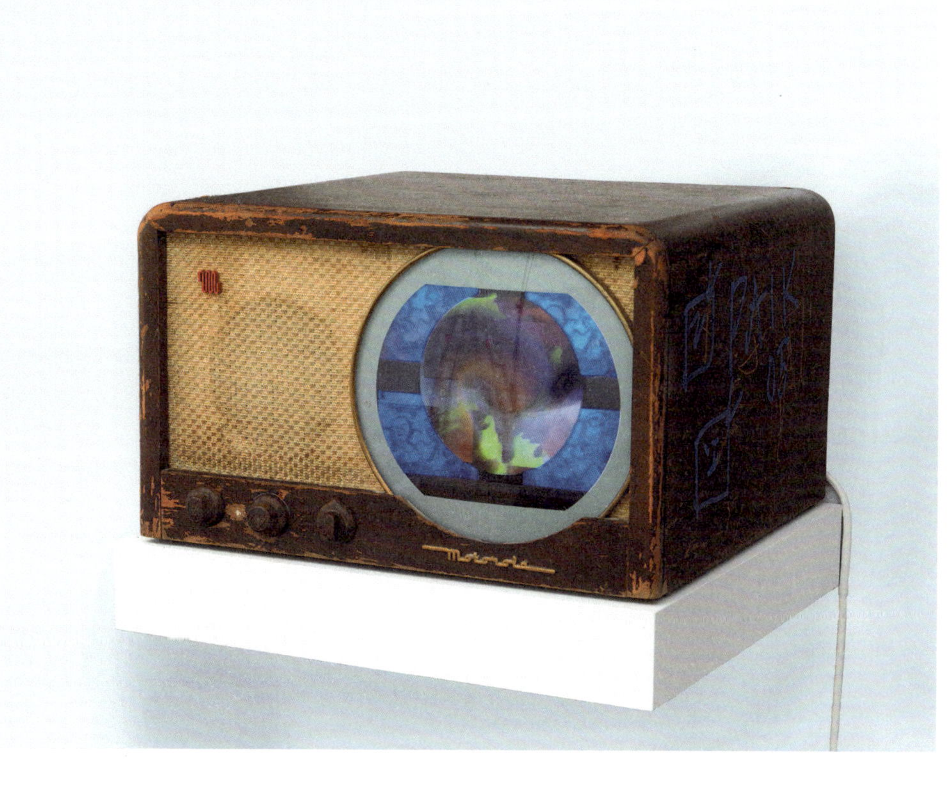

نـام جـون بايـك

(1932، كوريا الجنوبية – 2006،
الولايات المتحدة الأمريكية)

تلفزيون واسع العين، 2005

NAM JUNE PAIK

(b. 1932, South Korea
d. 2006, USA)

Big Eye TV, 2005

Single-channel video (color, silent), acrylic and permanent
oil marker on a 13-in. monitor in a King Television cabinet
45.4 × 56.5 × 52.7 cm
© Nam June Paik Estate

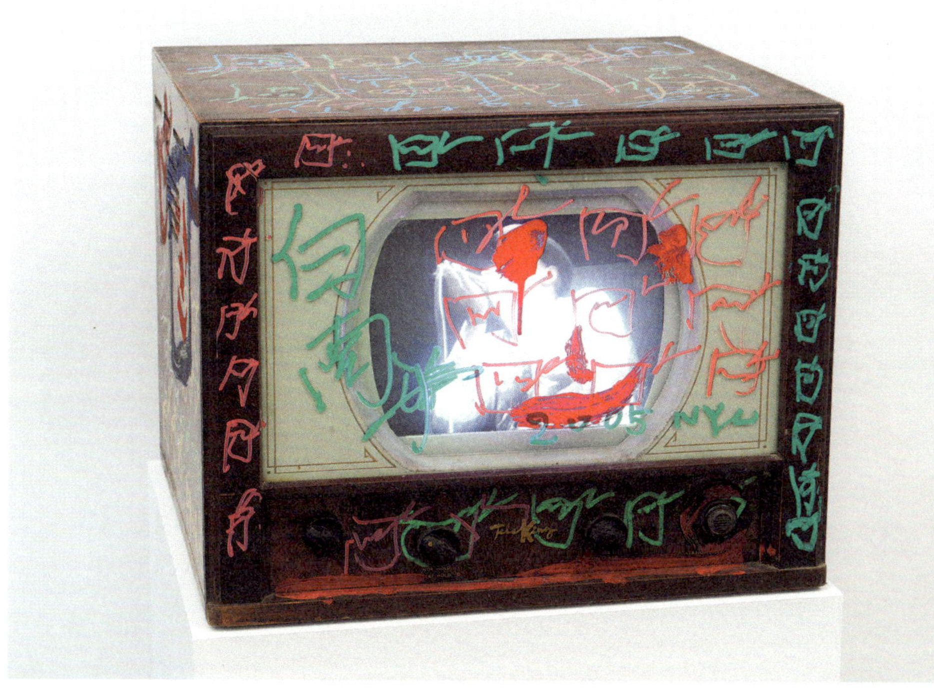

NAM JUNE PAIK

(b. 1932, South Korea
d. 2006, USA)

Admiral / Crying TV, 2005

Single-channel video (color, silent), acrylic and permanent oil marker on a 12-in. LCD monitor in a vintage television cabinet
37.8 × 40 × 49.8 cm
© Nam June Paik Estate

نــــام جــــون بايــــك

(1932، كوريا الجنوبية - 2006،
الولايات المتحدة الأمريكية)

الأميرال/التلفزيون الباكي، 2005

فيديـو أحادي القناة (ملون، صامت)، أكريليك وقلم عريض زيتي دائم
على شاشـة LCD مقاس 12 بوصة في خزانة تلفزيون عتيقة
37.8 × 40 × 49.9 سم
© تركة نام جون بايك

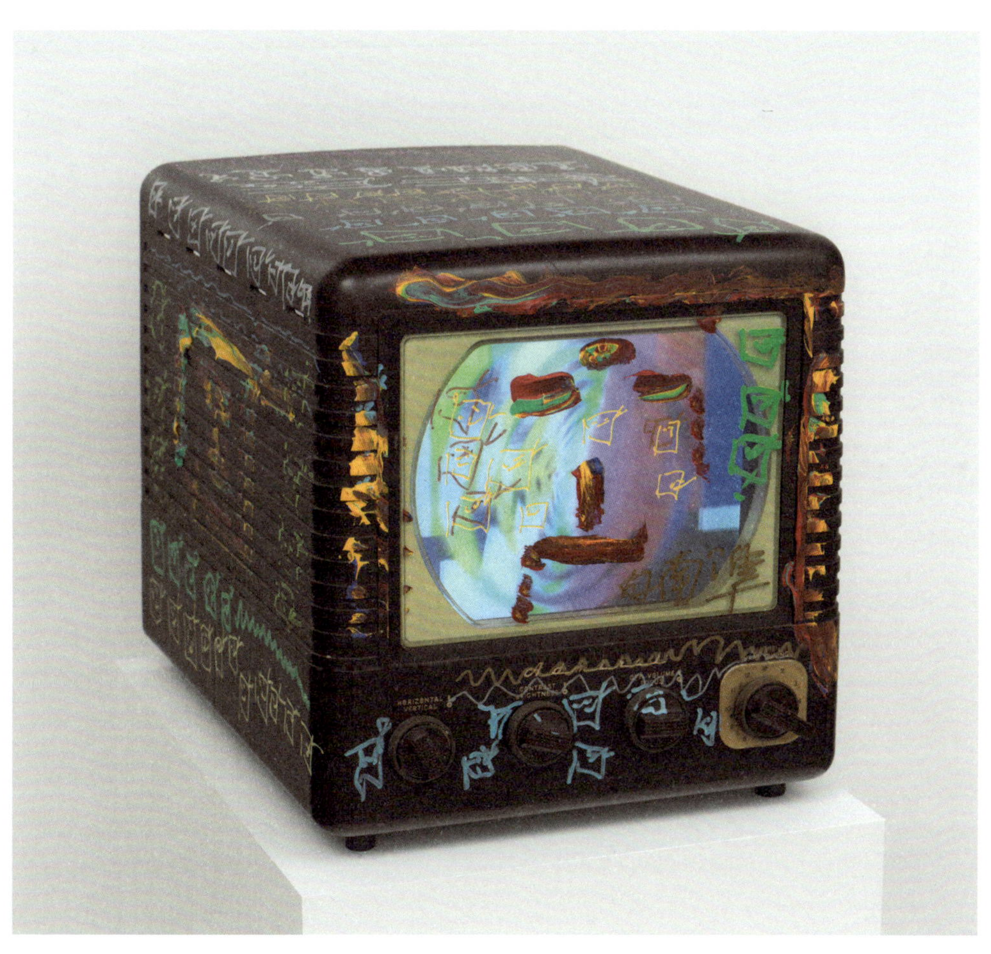

جـــون سالفيســــت

(مواليد 1955،
الولايات المتحدة الأمريكية)
يقيم ويعمل في فيلادلفيا
(الولايات المتحدة الأمريكية)

جون سالفيست فنانٌ معاصر ومفكر ومبدع وأستاذ سابق للفنون في جامعة ولاية أركنساس، حصل على درجة البكالوريوس في اللغة الإنجليزية من جامعة ديوك في عام 1977، وماجستير في الأدب الإنجليزي من جامعة أيوا في عام 1979، وماجستير في الفنون الجميلة في النحت من جامعة أيوا في عام 1983، وظهرت أعماله في العديد من المنشورات، ومن أبرزها Art in America وThe New York Times وThe Village Voice وArt Papers وThe New Art Examiner، ويتعمق سالفيست من خلال أعماله وتركيباته المتكيفة مع المواقع، في موضوعات الزمن والموت، وغالباً ما يستخدم الأدب والنصوص واللغة كوسائل متعددة التفسيرات، مستكشفاً العلاقة المعقدة بين العناصر النصية والأشياء اليومية.

شارك في العديد من المعارض الجماعية في جميع أنحاء الولايات المتحدة الأمريكية، ومن أبرزها جناح غاليري ديفيد لوسك في معرض شيكاغو للفنون (2024)؛ "XX: معرض العشرين عاماً" في غاليري مورغان ليمان، نيويورك (2022)؛ "تيك تاك: الوقت في الفن المعاصر" في قاعة الفنون في كلية ليمان، برونكس (2018)؛ "الفن الآن" في قاعة هيرست في برج هيرست، نيويورك (2017)؛ "حالة الفن: اكتشاف الفن الأمريكي الآن" في متحف كريستال بريدجز للفن الأمريكي، بنتونفيل (2014)؛ "الطقوس والبقايا: فن الشرب" في متحف KMAC للفن المعاصر، لويزفيل (2014)؛ "إنتروبانغ" في غاليري SPACE، بورتلاند (2009)؛ "أريد الحلوى" في متحف نهر هدسون، يونكرز (2007)؛ "فضاء الطيور: الطيور في أعمال الفنانين ما بعد حركة

أودوبون" في مركز الفنون المعاصرة، نيو أورلينز (2004)؛ "ترينيالي نيو أورليانز في متحف نيو أورليانز للفنون (1998)؛ "تجميع" في مركز ساوث إيسترن للفن المعاصر، وينستون سالم (1992)؛ بينالي بروكس في متحف بروكس للفنون، ممفيس (1992). أما معارضه الفردية في الولايات المتحدة الأمريكية فتشمل "تكرارات" في غاليري ديفيد لوسك، ممفيس (2023)؛ "انكسار" في غاليري SITE، هيوستن (2017)؛ "BassX: جون سالفيست" في متحف باس للفنون، ميامي (2016)؛ "دروس الأشياء" في غاليري مورجان ليمان، نيويورك (2014)؛ "قرن الوفرة الجديد وسند الإدانة الكبير" في قاعة غراند للفنون، كانساس سيتي (2011)؛ "طيران إلخ." في غاليري بيرنيس شتاينباوم، ميامي (2005)؛ "جون سالفيست: TEXTure" في متحف أركنساس للفنون الجميلة، ليتل روك (2002)؛ "جون سالفيست: الوقت بين يديه" في متحف فينيكس للفنون (1999)؛ "لا شيء يدوم" في متحف الفن المعاصر الجديد، نيويورك (1998)؛ "تأمل 7.21" في متحف الفن المعاصر، سانت لويس (1997)؛ "جرد" قاعة البلدية للفنون في تشاستين، أتلانتا (1996)؛ "جون سالفيست: نحت" في مركز سالينا للفنون (1995).

علاوة على ذلك، حاز سالفيست على العديد من الجوائز، من بينها زمالات الصندوق الوطني للفنون في عامي 1991 و1993، ومنحة مؤسسة بولوك-كراسنر في عام 1998، وزمالات مجلس الفنون بالولاية من نيوجيرسي وأركنساس. وقد أكمل العديد من المشاريع العامة الدائمة في مركز كانون للفنون المسرحية بممفيس ومطار هارتسفيلد جاكسون الدولي في أتلانتا، بالإضافة إلى عدد من المشاريع العامة المؤقتة، من بينها "إعطاء أهمية كبيرة لشبكة العين" في سبرينغديل (2017)، و"IOU/USA" في كانساس سيتي (2011).

JOHN SALVEST

(b. 1955, USA)
Lives and works in
Philadelphia, USA

John Salvest is a contemporary artist, a former professor of art at Arkansas State University, a thinker, and a maker. He received his BA in English from Duke University in 1977; an MA in English literature from the University of Iowa in 1979; and an MFA in sculpture from the University of Iowa in 1983. The artist's work has been featured in various publications, such as *Art in America*, *The New York Times*, *The Village Voice*, *Art Papers*, and *The New Art Examiner*, among others. Through his site-specific installations and objects, Salvest delves into themes of time and mortality. He frequently employs literature, text, and language as vehicles for a multiplicity of interpretations, thereby fostering an exploration of the intricate relationship between textual elements and everyday objects.

The artist has participated in numerous group exhibitions throughout the USA, including David Lusk Gallery at Chicago Art Expo, (2024); *XX: Twenty Year Exhibition*, Morgan Lehman Gallery, New York (2022); *Tick-Tock: Time in Contemporary Art*, Lehman College Art Gallery, the Bronx (2018); *Art Now*, Hearst Galleries, Hearst Tower, New York (2017); *State of the Art: Discovering American Art Now*, Crystal Bridges Museum of American Art, Bentonville (2014); *Ritual & Residue: The Art of Drink*, KMAC Contemporary Art Museum, Louisville (2014); *Interrobang*, SPACE Gallery, Portland (2009); *I Want Candy*, the Hudson River Museum, Yonkers (2007); *Birdspace: A Post-Audubon Artists Aviary*, Contemporary Arts Center, New Orleans (2004); New Orleans Triennial,

New Orleans Museum of Art (1998); *Assemblage*, Southeastern Center for Contemporary Art, Winston-Salem (1992); and Brooks Biennial, Brooks Museum of Art, Memphis (1992); among others. Selected solo exhibitions in the USA include *Iterations*, David Lusk Gallery, Memphis (2023); *Breaking*, SITE Gallery, Houston (2017); *BassX: John Salvest*, Bass Museum of Art, Miami (2016); *Object Lessons*, Morgan Lehman Gallery, New York (2014); *New Cornucopia and the Big IOU*, Grand Arts, Kansas City (2011); *FLY etc.*, Bernice Steinbaum Gallery, Miami (2005); *John Salvest: TEXTure*, Arkansas Museum of Fine Arts, Little Rock (2002); *John Salvest: Time on His Hands*, Phoenix Art Museum (1999); *Nothing Endures*, New Museum of Contemporary Art, New York (1998); *Meditation 7.21*, Contemporary Art Museum, St. Louis (1997); *Inventory*, City Gallery at Chastain, Atlanta (1996); and *John Salvest: Sculpture*, Salina Art Center (1995).

Furthermore, Salvest has received numerous awards, including National Endowment for the Arts Fellowships in 1991 and 1993, a Pollock-Krasner Foundation Grant in 1998, and State Arts Council Fellowships from New Jersey and Arkansas. He has completed several permanent public projects, such as works for the Cannon Center for the Performing Arts in Memphis and Atlanta's Hartsfield-Jackson International Airport, as well as the temporary public projects *Too much importance has been given to the retinal*, Springdale, (2017), and *IOU/USA*, Kansas City (2011).

جـــــــون سالفيســــــت

(مواليد 1955، الولايات المتحدة الأمريكية)

الحبر المتلاشي، 2014

الصحف والصفائح المعدنية والمغناطيس
والخيوط الأحادية والخيوط
مقاسات مختلفة
بإذن من الفنان

JOHN SALVEST
(b. 1955, USA)

Disappearing Ink, 2014

Newspapers, metal sheet, magnets,
monofilament, and string
Dimensions variable
Courtesy of the artist

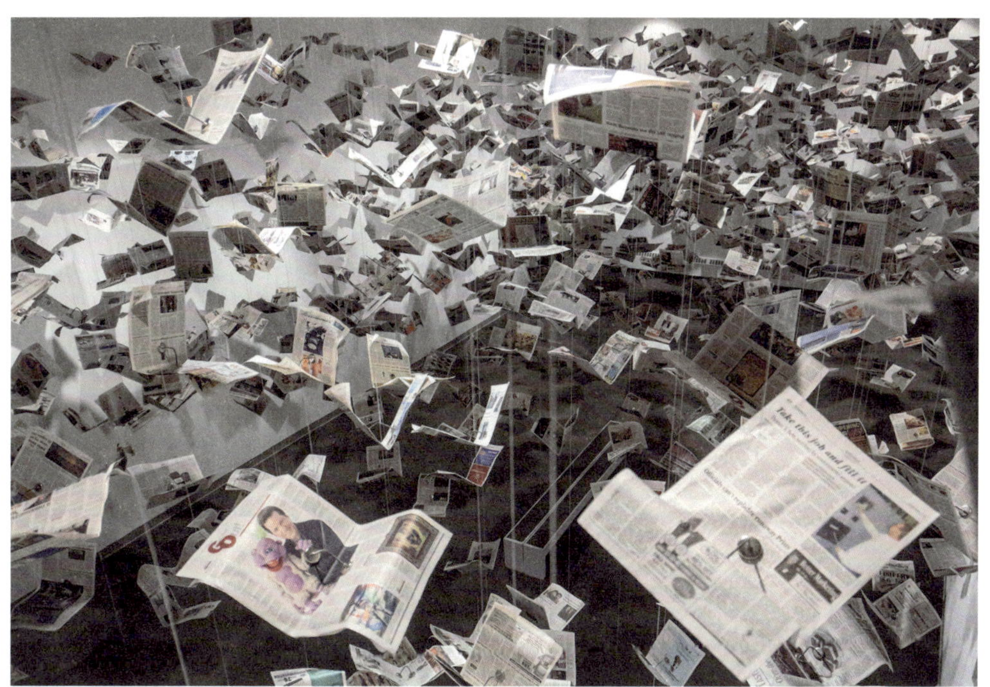

فيصـــل سـمـرة

(مواليد 1955، البحرين)
يقيم ويعمل بين المنامة
(البحرين). والدمام
(المملكة العربية السعودية)
وغرناطة (إسبانيا)

فيصل سمرة فنانٌ متعدد الوسائط يركز في أعماله على التصوير الرقمي والرسم والنحت والفيديو والأداء، مستكشفاً بذلك مختلف الموضوعات الوجودية؛ حصل على درجة البكالوريوس من المدرسة الوطنية العليا للفنون الجميلة في باريس، فرنسا عام 1980، وفي العام نفسه، أصبح مصمماً للديكور في التلفزيون السعودي، وسرعان ما شغل منصب كبير مصممي الجرافيك في شركة بكتل العربية في مدينة الجبيل الصناعية في المملكة العربية السعودية، ثم عمل بدوام جزئي لدى الرئاسة العامة لرعاية الشباب كمشرف عام على قسم الفنون التشكيلية في المنطقة الشرقية في المملكة العربية السعودية حتى عام 1983، وأسّس بعد ذلك شركة للتصميم الداخلي في الدمام، ولكنه انتقل بعد فترة وجيزة إلى فرنسا حيث عمل كمستشار في قسم الفنون التشكيلية والرسم في معهد العالم العربي، ثم أسس شركة للتصاميم الإسلامية والحرفية عملت في كل من المغرب والمملكة العربية السعودية، وفي عام 1995، أسّس غاليري "فيجن" في المنامة بالبحرين لتكون منبراً للفنانين الصاعدين في المنطقة. ومنذ منتصف الثمانينيات من القرن العشرين دفع سمرة حدود الوسائط الفنية، وزاول الفن من منظار التجريب والبحث وتعمّق على مر السنين في مفاهيم العفوية والديناميكية والسِّرّية.

عُرضت أعمال فيصل محلياً ودولياً؛ فقد شارك في العديد من المعارض الجماعية، من أبرزها بينالي الدرعية في المملكة العربية السعودية (2021)؛ وشارك بأعمال كـ "صورة زمنية: لمحة عامة لفن الفيديو في المملكة العربية السعودية" في غاليري أثر بجدة، المملكة العربية السعودية (2020)؛ و"وسم" في معهد مسك للفنون بالرياض، المملكة العربية السعودية (2020)؛ وبينالي

الجنوب في بوينس آيرس، الأرجنتين (2019)؛ و21,39 فن في جدة في المجلس الفني السعودي، المملكة العربية السعودية (2019)؛ وبينالي القاهرة، مصر (2018)؛ و"التخـوم" (بوردرلاند) في غاليري لو في سان دييغو، الولايات المتحدة الأمريكية (2016)؛ و"نظرة من الداخل: الفن العربي المعاصر (تصوير وفيديو ووسائط متعددة)" في غاليري قصر الإمارات بأبوظبي، الإمارات العربية المتحدة (2015)؛ والنسخة الأولى لمبادرة "حافة الجزيرة العربية" في لندن، المملكة المتحدة (2013)؛ و"تعالوا معاً"، حافة الجزيرة العربية، في غاليري أولد ترومان بلندن، المملكة المتحدة (2012)؛ بينالي برلين السادس، ألمانيا (2010)؛ و"كلمة في الفن: فنانو الشرق الأوسط الحديث" في المتحف البريطاني بلندن، المملكة المتحدة (2006)؛ و"مجموعة كنده للفن العربي المعاصر" في معهد العالم العربي بباريس، فرنسا (2002). وعلى مدى مسيرته الفنية، أقام فيصل سمرة أكثر من أربعين معرضاً فردياً، من بينها مشاركته في بينالي الإسكندرية، مصر (2019)؛ "الاحتباس الحراري" في عمارة بن مطر بالمحرّق، البحرين (2015)؛ و"شانتي" في غاليري إيتش دي بالدار البيضاء، المغرب (2012)؛ و"واقع مشوّه 3" في غاليري ناتالي أوباديا بباريس، فرنسا (2009)؛ و"جسـد آخر 2" في غاليري غرين آرت بدبي، الإمارات العربية المتحدة (2005)؛ و"أيقونة" في غاليري مسافة، الكويت (1998)؛ "آكت نوماد" في غاليري إتيان دينيه بباريس، فرنسا (1989).

دخلت أعماله إلى العديد من المجموعات الفنية الخاصة والعامة كمجموعة المتحف البريطاني في لندن، المملكة المتحدة؛ ومعهد العالم العربي في باريس، فرنسا؛ ومؤسسة جميل للفنون في دبي، الإمارات العربية المتحدة؛ ومؤسسة المنصورية في جدة، المملكة العربية السعودية؛ ومؤسسة خالد شومان في عمّان، الأردن؛ والمتحف العربي للفن الحديث في الدوحة، قطر؛ ومركز الملك عبد العزيز الثقافي العالمي "إثراء" بالظهران، المملكة العربية السعودية؛ ووزارة الثقافة السعودية.

FAISAL SAMRA

(b. 1955, Bahrain), Lives and works between Manama, Bahrain; Dammam, Saudi Arabia; and Granada, Spain

Faisal Samra is a multimedia artist who weaves various mediums, including digital photography, painting, sculpture, video, and performance, to explore existentialist themes. He earned a bachelor's degree from l'École nationale supérieure des Beaux-Arts in Paris, France in 1980. That same year, he became a stage designer for Saudi TV, and he soon went on to work as the senior graphic designer at Arabian Bechtel Co. in Jubail, Saudi Arabia. After this, he worked part-time with the Saudi Ministry of Youth Welfare as the general supervisor of the Fine Arts Department in the Eastern Region of Saudi Arabia until 1983. He then founded an interior design studio in Dammam, but shortly thereafter, he moved to France, where he worked as a consultant in the Fine Arts and Graphics division at the Institut du monde arabe, Paris. Following this, he established the Islamic & Artisan Design Company, which operated in both Morocco and Saudi Arabia, and in 1995, he also founded the Vision Gallery in Manama, Bahrain, providing a platform for emerging artists in the region. Since the mid-1980s, Samra has challenged the boundaries of media, meticulously approaching his art via experimentation and research. Over the years, his oeuvre has evolved, as he has delved into concepts of spontaneity, dynamism, and secrecy.

Samra's work has been exhibited locally and internationally. Select group exhibitions include Diriyah Biennale, Saudi Arabia (2021); *Durational Portrait: A Brief Overview of Video Art in Saudi Arabia*, Athr Gallery, Jeddah, Saudi Arabia (2020); *Imprint*, Misk Art Institute, Riyadh, Saudi Arabia (2020); Bienalsur, Buenos Aires, Argentina (2019); 21, 39 Jeddah Arts, Saudi Art Council, Saudi Arabia (2019); Cairo Biennale, Egypt (2018); *Borderland*, Low Gallery, San Diego, USA (2016); *View from Inside: Contemporary Arab Photography, Video and Mixed Media Art*, Emirates Palace Gallery, Abu Dhabi, UAE (2015); *Edition #1*, Edge of Arabia Gallery, London, UK (2013); *#COMETOGETHER*, Edge of Arabia, Old Truman Brewery London, UK (2012); 6th Berlin Biennale, Germany (2010); *Word into Art: Artists of the Modern Middle East*, British Museum, London, UK (2006); and the *Kinda Foundation Collection*, Institut du monde arabe, Paris, France (2002), among others. During his career, the artist has held more than forty solo exhibitions, including Alexandria Biennale, Egypt (2019); *Global Warming*, Bin Matar House, Muharraq, Bahrain (2015); *Shanty*, Galerie HD, Casablanca, Morocco (2012); *Distorted Reality III*, Galerie Nathalie Obadia, Paris, France (2009); *Other Body 2*, Green Art Gallery, Dubai, UAE (2005); *Icon*, Masafa Gallery, Kuwait (1998); and *Acte Nomade*, Galerie Étienne Dinet, Paris, France (1989).

His works are held in numerous private and public collections, including those of the British Museum, London, UK; the Institut du monde arabe, Paris, France; the Jameel Art Foundation, Dubai, UAE; the Al-Mansouria Foundation, Jeddah, Saudi Arabia; the Khalid Shoman Foundation, Amman, Jordan; Mathaf: Arab Museum of Modern Art, Doha, Qatar; the King Abdulaziz Center for World Culture—Ithra, Dhahran, Saudi Arabia; and the Ministry of Culture, Saudi Arabia.

FAISAL SAMRA

(b. 1955, Bahrain)

Earth to Earth, 2007

Video installation
3 min., 7 sec.
Ed. 5 + 1 A.P.
Courtesy of the artist and Ayyam Gallery, Dubai

فيصـــــل ســـمرة

(مواليد 1955، البحرين)

تراب إلى تراب، 2007

تركيب فني باستخدام الفيديو
3 دقائق و7 ثوان
خمس نسخ + نسخة فنية
بإذن من الفنان وأيام غاليري في دبي

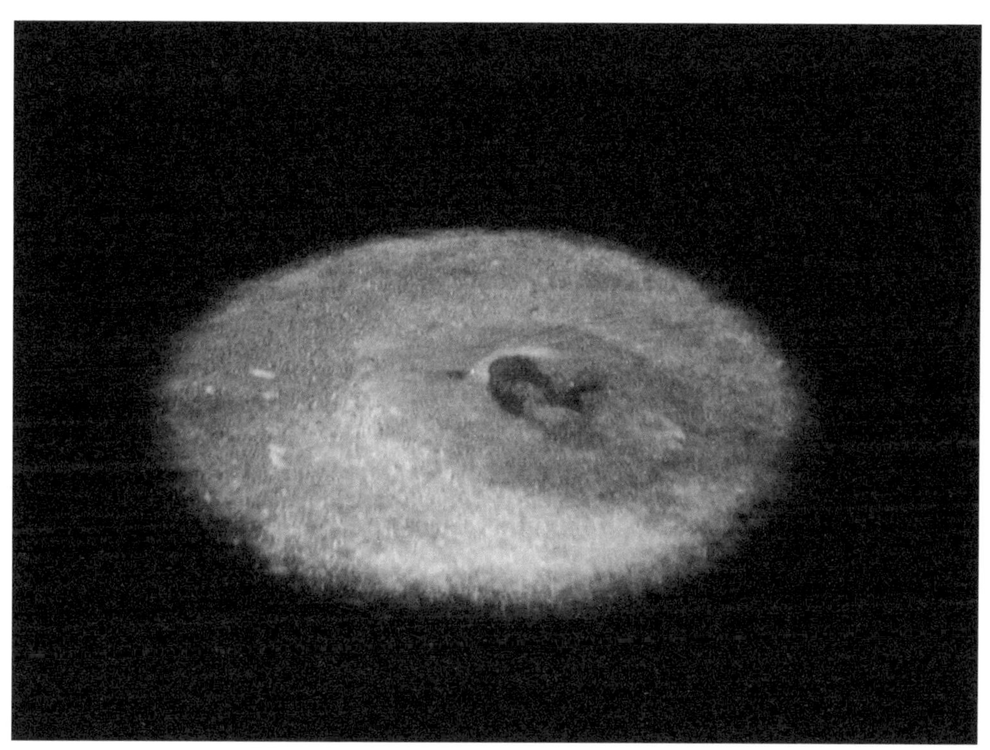

فيصـــل ســـمرة

(مواليد 1955، البحرين)

النظر في الحفرة، 2007

تركيب فني باستخدام الفيديو
8 دقائق و41 ثانية
خمس نسخ + نسخة فنية
بإذن من الفنان وأيام غاليري في دبي

FAISAL SAMRA

(b. 1955, Bahrain)

Looking In the Hole, 2007

Video installation
8 min., 41 sec.
Ed. 5 + 1 A.P
Courtesy of the artist and Ayyam Gallery, Dubai

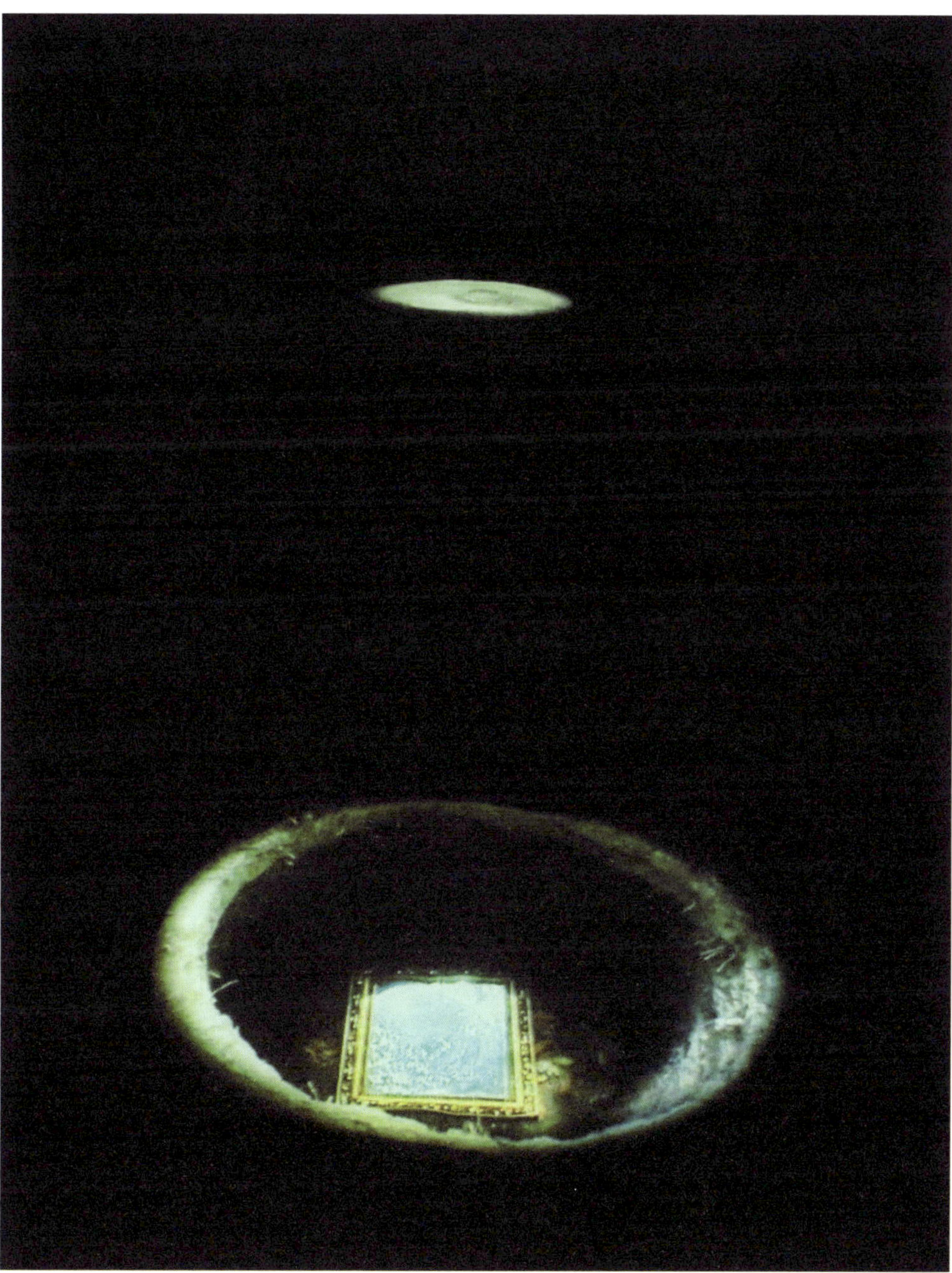

آنيــا ســليمان

(مواليد 1970، بولندا)
تقيم وتعمل في باريس (فرنسا)

آنيـا سـليمان فنانةٌ متعددة التخصصـات مصرية بولنديـة أمريكية، نشـأت فـي بغداد قبـل أن تغادر إلى الولايـات المتحـدة لإكمال دراسـتها، وتخرجت من جامعة هارفارد في عام 1992، ثم حصلت على درجة الماجسـتير مـن جامعـة كولومبيا. وانطلاقاً مـن خلفيتها الثقافيـة، دمجت في مزاولتها الفنية مختلف المقاربات العلمية والبحثية التي تنظر في العلاقات والوسائط والطبيعة والتكنولوجيا، وتسخّر فـي عملها مجموعة واسعة من الوسـائط كالرسـم والفيديو والنصـوص والتركيب والأداء، وتنطلق من الرسـم بالخطوط الرفيعة مستخدمةً تقنيات رسم الخرائط والتتبع والتلويـن والكتابة وتنضيد الحروف لإنشاء أعمال متعددة القراءات تعكس في تشكيلها الأفكار المتضاربة.

عُرضـت أعمـال آنيـا سـليمان فـي العديد من المعارض الجماعية، ومن أبرزها؛ "استشعار اللوحة: أعمال مـن المجموعـة الفنية لمؤسسـة بنك كوينو للإدخـار" فـي متحـف كاسـتيلو دي ريفولـي للفن المعاصـر بتورينـو، إيطاليـا (2023)؛ و"زمن الذات: اكتشـاف الذات المتطرفـة" في مركز جميـل للفنون بدبي، الإمـارات العربيـة المتحـدة (2021)؛ و"زمن لا مثيل لـه" فـي قاعـة بريغنـز للفنـون، النمسـا (2020)؛ و"تحـولات: دع كل شـيء يحـدث لـك" فـي متحـف كاسـتيلو دي ريفولـي بتورينـو، إيطاليا (2018)؛ و"مسـتأجرون" في متحف الفن المعاصر أنتويـرب، بلجيـكا (2015)؛ بينالي إسطنبول الرابع عشـر، تركيا (2015)؛ بينالي ويتنـي فـي متحف ويتني للفـن الأمريكي بنيويورك، الولايـات المتحدة الأمريكيـة (2010)؛ و"عندمـا يقول الفنانون نحن" فـي آرتيسـت سبيس بنيويورك، الولايـات المتحدة الأمريكيـة (2006)، ومـن بيـن معارضهـا الفردية

"تيرافـورم" فـي غاليـري صفيـر زملـر ببيـروت، لبنان (2022)؛ و"الطبيعـة تجربـة" فـي غاليـري آنجلـز ببرشلونة، إسبانيا (2019)؛ و"شرح الرقص للآلة" في غاليري صفير زملر بهامبورغ، ألمانيا (2017)؛ و"شبه المتوحـش" فـي متحـف الثقافـات ببازل، سويسـرا (2014)؛ و"المخاطـر البيولوجيـة" في مركز الرسم بنيويـورك، الولايـات المتحدة الأمريكيـة (2000).

ANIA SOLIMAN

(b. 1970, Poland)
Lives and works in Paris,
France

Ania Soliman is an Egyptian, Polish, and American interdisciplinary artist who grew up in Baghdad before leaving for the USA to complete her studies. She graduated from Harvard University in 1992, and then received her MA from Columbia University four years later. Fueled by her cultural background, her practice incorporates both scientific and research-based approaches that question relationships, media, nature, and technology. The artist works across a wide range of media, including drawing, video, text, installation, and performance. Using line drawing as a foundation, she employs techniques such as mapping, tracing, coloring, lettering, and embellishing to create layered works that often reflect conflicting ideas as they evolve.

Soliman's work has been exhibited in numerous group exhibitions, including *Sensing Painting: Works from the Art Collection of the Fondazione CRC*, Castello di Rivoli Museum of Contemporary Art, Turin, Italy (2023); *Age of You: A Kaleidoscopic Exploration of the Extreme Self*, Jameel Arts Centre, Dubai, UAE (2021); *Unprecedented Times*, Kunsthaus Bregenz, Austria (2020); *Metamorphoses: Let Everything Happen to You*, Castello Di Rivoli, Turin, Italy (2018); Lodgers, M HKA (Museum of Contemporary Art Antwerp), Belgium (2015); the 14th Istanbul Biennial, Turkey (2015); the Whitney Biennial, Whitney Museum of American Art, New York, USA (2010); and *When Artists Say We*, Artists Space, New York, USA (2006). Select solo exhibitions include *Terraform*, Sfeir-Semler Gallery Beirut, Lebanon (2022); *Nature is an Experiment*, àngels barcelona, Barcelona, Spain (2019); *Explaining Dance to a Machine*, Sfeir-Semler Gallery, Hamburg, Germany (2017); *Semiwild*, Museum der Kulturen Basel, Switzerland (2014); and *Biohazards*, The Drawing Center, New York, USA (2000), among others.

ANIA SOLIMAN

(b. 1970, Poland)

*Terraform 1
(everyone-zoospore, recovery-whew),
2022*

Colored pencil, encaustic and acrylic ink on paper
Four panels, 280 × 115 cm each
Courtesy of the artist and Sfeir-Semler Gallery,
Beirut and Hamburg

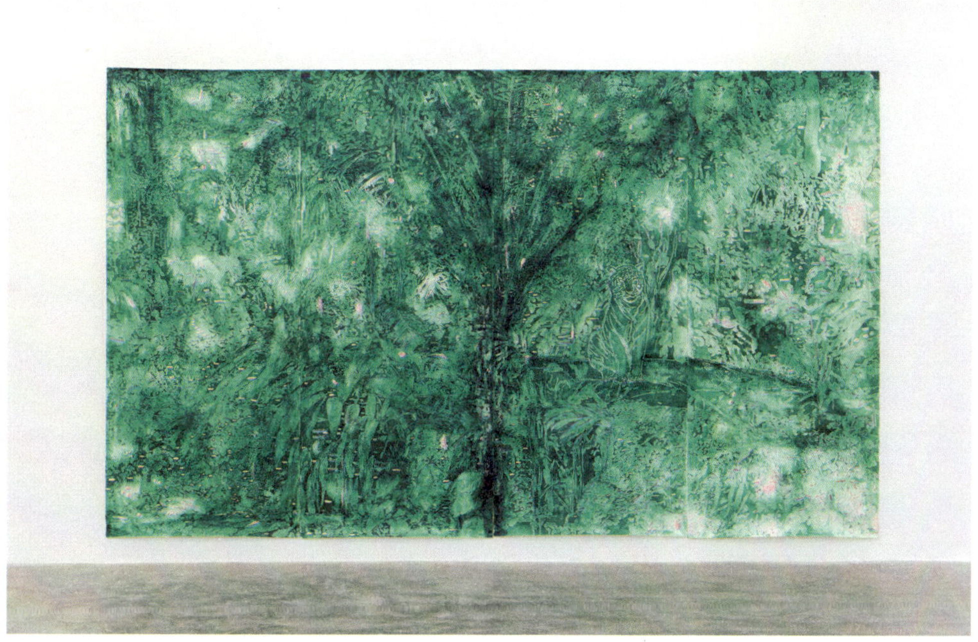

عصـــــــر الأثـــــر الخافــــــت
THE SILENT AGE OF SINGULARITY

Curator
Basma Alshathry, Director of Curatorial Department
and Chief Curator at Misk Art Institute

Assistant Curator
Aram Alajaji, Assistant Curator at Misk Art Institute

Exhibition Designer
Badr Zabarah, Senior Exhibition Designer
at Misk Art Institute

Authors
Aram Alajaji
Abdullah Alghathami
Basma Alshathry
Eiman Elgibreen

Editorial Coordination
Aram Alajaji

Translations
Moussa Alhouchi
Omar Odeh

Copyediting
Abdulrahman Sidi, Senior Editor at Misk Art Intitute
Eti Bonn-Muller

Special thanks to the artists, galleries, collectors
and institutions for their invaluable contributions.

القيم الفني
بسمة الشري، مدير عام إدارة التقييم الفني وكبير
القيمين الفنيين في معهد مسك للفنون

القيم الفني المساعد
آرام العجاجـي، القيـم الفني المسـاعد فـي معهد
مسـك للفنون

مصمم المعرض
بدر زباره، مصمم المعارض في معهد مسك للفنون

المؤلفون
آرام العجاجي
عبدالله الغذامي
بسمة الشري
إيمان الجبرين

تنسيق التحريري
آرام العجاجي

الترجمة
موسى الحوشي
عمر عودة

التدقيق اللغوي
عبد الرحمن سيدي، محرر أول في معهد مسك للفنون
إيتي بون-مولر

شكر خاص للفنانين والغاليريات والمقتنين
والمؤسسات على مساهماتهم القيمة.

Book Design and Layout
-scope Ateliers

English Proofreading
Zeina Assaf

First edition, 2024
© Kaph Books, 2024
© Misk Art Institute, 2024

ISBN: 978-614-8035-83-8

Printed in October 2024

Published by

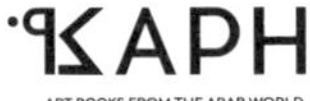

www.kaphbooks.com

Distribution
NORTH AMERICA - LATIN AMERICA - ASIA - AUSTRALIA
ARTBOOK | D.A.P.
75 Broad Street, Suite 630
New York, NY 10004
www.artbook.com

FRANCE - SWITZERLAND - BELGIUM - LUXEMBOURG
Les Presses du Réel
35 rue Colson,
21000 Dijon, France
www.lespressesdureel.com

REST OF EUROPE
Idea Books
Nieuwe Herengracht 11
1011 RK Amsterdam, The Netherlands
www.ideabooks.nl

MIDDLE EAST
CIEL BOOK DISTRIBUTION
Al Manara Road, Al Quoz 1, P.O.Box 282005
Dubai United Arab Emirates
www.ciel.me

تصميم الكتاب وتنسيقه
-سكوب أتلييه

المراجعة اللغوية العربية
محمد حمدان

الطبعة الأولى، 2024
© كتب كيف، 2024
© معهد مسك للفنون، 2024

ردمك: 978-614-8035-83-8

طُبع في أكتوبر 2024

النشر من قبل

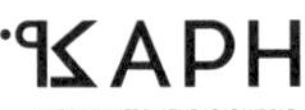

www.kaphbooks.com

التوزيع
أمريكا الشمالية - أمريكا اللاتينية - آسيا - أستراليا
ARTBOOK | D.A.P.
75 شارع برود، جناح 630
نيويورك، نيويورك 10004
www.artbook.com

فرنسا - سويسرا - بلجيكا - لوكسمبورغ
Les Presses du Réel
35 شارع كولسون،
21000 ديجون، فرنسا
www.lespressesdureel.com

بقية أوروبا
Idea Books
نيووي هيرنغراخت 11
1011 RK أمستردام، هولندا
www.ideabooks.nl

الشرق الأوسط
CIEL BOOK DISTRIBUTION
شارع المنارة، القوز 1، ص.ب 282005
دبي، الإمارات العربية المتحدة
www.ciel.me